THE

FRENCH
MARKET

COOKBOOK

ALSO BY CLOTILDE DUSOULIER

Chocolate & Zucchini

*Clotilde's Edible
Adventures in Paris*

THE FRENCH MARKET COOKBOOK

VEGETARIAN RECIPES
FROM MY PARISIAN KITCHEN

Clotilde Dusoulier

OF CHOCOLATEANDZUCCHINI.COM

CLARKSON POTTER/PUBLISHERS
NEW YORK

Library of Congress Cataloging-in-Publication Data is
available upon request.

ISBN 978-0-307-98482-1
eISBN 978-0-307-98483-8

Printed in China

Book and cover design by Rae Ann Spitzenberger
Front cover photography © Maridav (background) and
ingwervanille (food)
Food styling by Virginie Michelin

10 9 8 7 6 5 4 3 2 1

First Edition

For Milan,
who came along
for the ride

CONTENTS

ABOUT THIS BOOK

À propos de ce livre

I am a resolutely vegetable-oriented cook. I grew up in a family in which the seasonality of produce was such a cause for celebration that we made a wish every time we ate the first cherry, or the first pear or grape, of the season. To this day, the ebb and flow of the seasons moves me, and nothing makes my heart flutter like the first, and the last, of any fruit or vegetable.

Ever since I started to cook in my early twenties, having freshly moved out of my parents' house in Paris to work in California, meal planning has always begun with the question, "What's in the vegetable bin?" or "What looks good at the farmers' market?"

Gradually, over the past few years, meat and fish have become a smaller part of the equation as my combined interests in food, health, and the environment have led me to adopt a flexitarian diet: one that is predominantly vegetarian, with limited use of dairy products, and only occasional consumption of meat and fish.

It is not an easy stance to assume in France.

In classic French cuisine, as for most French home cooks, animal protein remains the foundation on which a meal is constructed; take it away and everything collapses.

But there is a lot more to French food than classic French cuisine; there is regional cooking, too, as developed over the centuries in each of France's provinces. These diverse cuisines reflect the typical peasant diet, high in plant-based foods and resourceful about using the local bounty, which varies widely, a function of different climates and geographical constraints.

Fortunately, a new generation of French chefs is devoting an increasing amount of attention to the vegetables they cook with; some of them care so much they've started their own vegetable gardens to follow their produce from seed to plate. And as other cooks and eaters are choosing to distance themselves from the domination of animal protein and explore alternatives, we are all coming to the same realization: This way of eating is not a limitation but rather a broadening of our food horizon, prompting us to discover new flavors and techniques.

In this book I offer my take on the love affair between French cuisine and vegetables. The colorful seasonal dishes I feature draw upon the regional French repertoire, borrow ideas from restaurant meals I've enjoyed, and combine them with my own inspirations, sparked by appetite or opportunity.

Whatever your food philosophy, whether you're an omnivore, a "lessmeatarian" (a term coined by writer Mark Bittman), a flexitarian, a vegetarian, or a vegan, I hope you'll grab an apron, join me by the stove, and help me chop some herbs as I tell you about these dishes.

HOW TO SHOP FOR PRODUCE

If you work with glowingly fresh, seasonally grown produce, the cooking process will feel natural and effortless and you'll be rewarded with vibrant flavors and appetizing looks. That's a promise.

If, on the other hand, you make do with mass-cultivated produce that's been grown out of season, pumped with chemicals, picked before it's had a chance to ripen, and driven or flown in refrigerated containers for a great distance, no amount of cooking skills can fix that situation.

That's why learning how to cook should really begin with learning how to shop.

First identify the best source of produce available to you. If you have access to a farmer's market or a community-supported agriculture (CSA) delivery service, or if you're able to grow some of your own produce, you're in luck. If not, it is

About the use (or overuse) of cheese

It's not hard to come up with hearty meatless dishes that are made substantial by simply slapping on a hefty dose of cheesy goodness. But it is not a creative way to envision a plant-based meal nor is it desirable from a nutritional perspective, so I have chosen to highlight recipes that go easy on the cheese.

worth exploring different grocery stores in your area to see which stock the freshest produce. Don't hesitate to express your wishes to the store manager; it may not change the situation overnight, but at least you'll have done your part.

Whatever the source, the key to shopping for produce is to avoid going with a list that you follow rigidly. Instead, go with your eyes and mind wide open and let yourself be surprised and seduced by the ingredients. Browse around, see what looks good and fresh and vibrant, and pick that up. Once you're home, you'll figure out how best to prepare it.

Throughout the book I've included advice on how to select specific vegeta-bles. Even if you feel you're an inexperienced produce shopper, you'll soon learn to trust your sight and your touch. Think of selecting flowers at the florist: You can tell the difference between a recently cut, glowingly fresh peony and one that's a few days old, its petals fraying at the edges, its head lolling to the side. Right? Well, it's not so different here: Seek out vegetables that look perky and alert, with intense colors and no discolored or soft spots.

There is one nonnegotiable caveat, whether or not you shop intuitively: You need to buy a combination of produce that keeps and produce that doesn't. If you go on a weekly produce run, which is ideal, you should aim to buy two to three days'

worth of fragile vegetables and fill the rest of your basket with sturdier ones that will last until the end of the week at least.

Neglecting this rule leads directly to the feelings of guilt and despair that seize all of us when we open the fridge only to be faced with moldy arugula and limp carrots.

Depending on how many times you guesstimate you'll eat at home over the next week, you'll want to mix and match among the following groups of produce:

Fragile (use within two days): artichokes, asparagus, berries, cherries, fava beans, figs, green beans, green peas, leafy fresh herbs, melon (if ripe), mushrooms, scallions, small salad leaves, Swiss chard leaves

Somewhat sturdy (use within four days to a week, checking them daily): apricots, bell peppers, broccoli, Brussels sprouts, cauliflower, cucumber, eggplant, endives, fennel, grapes, heads of lettuce, kiwifruit, kohlrabi, nectarines, peaches, pears, plums, quinces, radishes, shell beans, spinach, Swiss chard stalks, summer squash

Sturdy (use within two weeks): apples, beets, cabbages, carrots, celery, celery root, citrus fruits, ginger, Jerusalem artichokes, parsnips, potatoes, rutabagas, salsify, tomatoes, turnips, winter squash

Long storage (use within a few months): dried fruits, garlic, nuts, onions, shallots

CREATING VEGETABLE-FOCUSED MEALS

Variety is key in creating any dish or planning a menu. For optimal satisfaction, you want to juxtapose different types of flavors (sweet, salty, tart, meaty, savory, bitter, grassy, nutty, acidic, caramelized, woody, smoky, earthy . . .) and textures (soft, crisp, creamy, slippery, chewy, crunchy, tender, grainy, fluffy . . .). You also want to highlight foods of different colors and alternate between the cooked and the raw, the warm and the cold, the comforting and the unusual, so a dish never falls into monotony.

These principles are true under any circumstances and, with a little experience, cooks follow them intuitively. But you should keep them at the forefront of your mind if you've recently made the switch to working with more vegetables and other plant-based ingredients; you'll have to learn to re-create those pleasing variations using a different set of tools.

The recipes in this book are all built this way; I invite you to tag along and discover the exciting possibilities that the vegetable realm offers.

GLACES *Berthillon* Café   Restaurant   7J/7

SPRING
Le printemps

As tender greens and waxy pods pile up on market stalls, all I want to do is prop my basket open and let young and sprightly things tumble in. Spring is the season of effortless inspiration in the kitchen.

But spring in Paris comes in fits and starts, the weather alternating between golden days and chilly dips. And so my spring repertoire offers the kind of bright dishes I crave on promisingly sunny days, when it feels like winter has truly departed, and also comforting ones to lean into when it turns out the season's influence lingers still.

Regardless of where my recipes fall in this dichotomy, they're a celebration of the produce of spring, from the pop of pea pods to the snap of asparagus—and the uncontainable excitement their appearance brings.

PRODUCE TO PLAY WITH IN THE SPRING

- Artichokes
- Asparagus
- Beets
- Carrots
- Dandelions

- Fava beans
- Garlic
- Green peas
- Kohlrabi
- Lettuce

- Mâche
- Morels
- New potatoes
- Onions

- Radishes
- Rhubarb
- Scallions
- Sorrel
- Spinach

- Strawberries
- Swiss chard
- Turnips
- Watercress

AVOCADO AND RADISH MINI-TARTINES

Mini-tartines radis et avocat

The classic French way of eating radishes, and the way I've eaten them since childhood, is as an hors d'oeuvre: You trim the radishes, leaving a short tuft of stem as a little handle to pick them up, and serve them with chilled salted butter and fresh baguette.

The combination of radish, butter, salt, and bread seems like it can't be improved upon, except perhaps if you replace the butter with avocado, which I think of as vegetable butter. For these quick mini-*tartines,* I season the avocado with lemon juice, cumin, and salt, mash it onto slim slices of baguette, and scatter paper-thin slices of pink radishes on top, like oversized confetti. Bright in color and flavor, they're a favorite spring nibble to accompany an early evening drink at my house.

1. Scoop the avocado flesh into a bowl. Add the lemon juice, cumin, and salt and season with pepper and hot sauce (if using). Mash the avocado roughly to get a slightly chunky texture. Taste and adjust the seasoning; it should be so zesty you have to resist eating the whole bowl with a spoon.

2. Slice the baguette at an angle into ½-inch / 1 cm slices and spread the slices with the mashed avocado.

3. Using a mandoline slicer or very sharp knife, slice the radishes crosswise into paper-thin rounds. Scatter on top of the avocado, sprinkle with a touch more salt, and serve.

SERVES 4 TO 6

2 **avocados** (each about 7 ounces / 200 g)

4 teaspoons freshly squeezed **lemon juice**

1 teaspoon ground **cumin**

½ teaspoon **fine sea salt,** plus more for sprinkling

Freshly ground **black pepper**

Hot sauce (optional)

1 slim **baguette**

A bunch or two of small **pink** or **red radishes** (about 24 small), trimmed

1 pound / 450 g green asparagus

Fine sea salt

1⅓ cups / 200 g shelled green peas, fresh or frozen

12 large romaine lettuce leaves

1 tablespoon cold-pressed hazelnut oil or untoasted sesame oil

1 tablespoon neutral-tasting oil, such as grapeseed or safflower

1 tablespoon freshly squeezed lemon juice

Freshly ground black pepper

1 cup / 20 g chopped fresh chervil or cilantro leaves

½ recipe Blanch-Roasted New Potatoes (page 23), slightly warm

½ cup / 60 g hazelnuts, toasted (see page 68) and roughly chopped

VERY GREEN SALAD
Salade toute verte

Spring is the season I most closely associate with the color green—and the irresistible craving for it on my plate. I am especially fond of combining different shades of green in salads such as this one: the baby green of a romaine lettuce, the peppy green of fresh peas, and the darker emerald of asparagus, all punctuated by bright flecks of leafy herbs.

The only exception to the color scheme here is the addition of hazelnuts, which bring a welcome toasty crunch, and roasted new potatoes, which turn this salad into a full meal.

The naming of the salad is a nostalgic nod to Le Délicabar, the much-missed restaurant once housed in Le Bon Marché, a department store in Paris, which offered an array of color-themed salads on its menu: *salade toute violette, salade toute orange,* and *salade toute blanche,* among other vegetable-focused dishes.

1. Trim the bottom of the asparagus stalks, just to remove the woody part. Cut the stalks at an angle into ½-inch / 1 cm slices, leaving the tips whole.

2. Set up a steamer. Sprinkle the asparagus with salt and steam, tightly covered, until cooked through but still with a little bite, 4 to 5 minutes. Set aside to cool. Steam the peas in the same fashion.

3. Cut the leaves of lettuce in half along their central spine, then cut at an angle into ½-inch / 1 cm strips. You should get about 8 cups, loosely packed.

4. In a large salad bowl, whisk together both oils, the lemon juice, and ½ teaspoon salt.

5. Just before serving, add the lettuce to the dressing, sprinkle with pepper, and toss to coat. Fold in the asparagus, peas, chervil, and warm potatoes.

6. Divide among 4 salad bowls, sprinkle with the hazelnuts, and serve.

SERVES 4

1 cup / 200 g
French green lentils

1 bay leaf

½ small yellow onion
(2¼ ounces / 60 g),
finely chopped

Fine sea salt

4½ ounces / 130 g
pink or red radishes
and/or kohlrabi,
trimmed and diced

1 teaspoon Dijon
mustard

1 tablespoon plus
1 teaspoon cider
vinegar

1 tablespoon plus
2 teaspoons extra-
virgin olive oil

Freshly ground
black pepper

½ cup / 20 g
chopped fresh chives

8 fresh mint leaves,
finely chopped

7 ounces / 200 g
watercress
(about 8 cups)

1 teaspoon mild
honey

CRUNCHY LENTIL AND WATERCRESS SALAD

Salade croquante de lentilles et cresson

This salad is inspired by a dish served at BAL Café, a popular restaurant tucked away in a quiet dead-end street behind Place de Clichy in Paris. The area has yet to become gentrified so it's an unlikely yet lovely place to lunch; it is bright and modern and the wide windows look out onto a tiny public park across the alley.

One day in early spring, I ate there with a friend who ordered braised pork cheeks, which were served over a lentil salad with a few branches of watercress. The combination of mustardy lentils and piquant watercress stuck with me, and my appetite brings me back to it as long as watercress graces market stalls.

I add diced radishes and kohlrabi for freshness, color, and crunch, as well as finely chopped mint and chives. The lentil salad can be made in advance, but dress the watercress close to serving time so it won't wilt. Serve with toasted slices of country bread, if desired.

1. Rinse the lentils and put them with the bay leaf and onion in a medium saucepan. Add 1½ cups / 360 ml cold water, cover, and bring to a simmer over medium heat. Simmer for 15 minutes. Add ½ teaspoon salt and simmer until the lentils are cooked through but still have a little bite, about 5 minutes. Drain, rinse with fresh water, and set aside for 10 minutes to cool.

2. Put the cooled lentils in a medium salad bowl. Add the radishes, mustard, 1 tablespoon of the cider vinegar, and 1 tablespoon of the olive oil. Sprinkle with salt and

RECIPE CONTINUES

pepper and toss to combine. Fold in the herbs, taste, and adjust the seasoning. This can be assembled a few hours ahead; cover and refrigerate until 30 minutes before serving.

3. Just before serving, dress the watercress: In a medium salad bowl, whisk together the remaining 1 teaspoon cider vinegar, 2 teaspoons olive oil, the honey, ½ teaspoon salt, and a generous grind from the pepper mill. Add the watercress and toss gently to coat. Taste and adjust the seasoning.

4. Divide the watercress among 4 salad bowls or plates, creating a slight depression in the middle, and spoon in the lentil salad.

KOHLRABI

Kohlrabi belongs to the cabbage family; in fact, it is sometimes sold as cabbage turnip. It has a plump, round, pastel-green body with graceful little arms shooting up from all sides and twirling around, ending in large green leaves. The greens are edible and may be used like parsley, while the vegetable itself can be trimmed of any rough spots, sliced thinly, and eaten raw, with a little salt sprinkled on top.

WATERCRESS

Watercress is a nutritious, peppery green from the mustard family that is grown in freshwater ponds and sold in attractive little bouquets. Trim the bottom of the stems; unless the stalks seem tough, they are edible. Beyond using it in salads, I also like to use watercress in soup or pesto and as a garnish in sandwiches.

BLANCH-ROASTED NEW POTATOES

Pommes de terre nouvelles rôties

SERVES 4

2 pounds / 900 g new potatoes (such as creamers or fingerlings), small and evenly sized, scrubbed

1 tablespoon coarse salt

2 tablespoons olive oil for cooking

1 teaspoon fleur de sel or other flaky salt

Freshly ground black pepper

The French have a particular fetish for new potatoes, those egg-smooth, thin-skinned, tender spuds that are in season in the spring. The most prized varieties come in pretty crates with a proudly displayed pedigree—*ratte du Touquet, bonotte de Noirmoutier*—while others are sold under the generic name of *grenaille* (lead shot) to indicate their very small size.

The skin on such young potatoes is tender and edible and the flesh inside is creamy and nutty. My cooking method of choice for these spuds makes the most of these two qualities: I parboil the potatoes and then roast them in the oven. Not only does this simple two-step cooking process ensure that the potatoes are creamy inside and will brown well, but it also shortens the overall baking time. The resulting golden and lightly wrinkled nuggets are nice in a salad (such as the Very Green Salad, page 18) or on their own with a drizzle of Herbed Tahini Sauce (page 214).

1. Preheat the oven to 425°F. / 220°C.

2. Put the potatoes in a medium saucepan, pour in cold water just to cover, and add the coarse salt. Cover and bring to a boil over medium-high heat. As soon as the water boils, drain the potatoes thoroughly and transfer to a baking dish large enough to accommodate them in a single layer. Drizzle with the olive oil, sprinkle with the fleur de sel, and toss well to coat.

3. Bake until cooked through, golden brown, and crusty, 30 to 40 minutes. Sprinkle with pepper and serve hot, slightly warm, or at room temperature.

SERVES 4

4 globe artichokes

**Classic Vinaigrette
(page 206)**

GLOBE ARTICHOKES WITH VINAIGRETTE
Artichauts vinaigrette

Fresh globe artichokes appeared regularly on the dinner table at my parents' house during the peak season, from May till July. My mother would cook four big *artichauts* from Brittany in the pressure cooker and whisk up a thick vinaigrette to serve as a dipping sauce. We ate the artichokes with our fingers, leaf by leaf, dipping them lightly in the vinaigrette, scraping the sweet flesh from the tips with our teeth, and tossing the leaves into a large bowl in the center of the table.

When I was very young, I seemed to find this all too much work and usually lost interest shortly before reaching the heart of the artichoke, the tastiest part. I know better now, savoring the experience and wondering when I'll reach the point where the leaves grow more and more tender. When I finally push away the dome of hay-like fibers that protect the heart, I get a special thrill knowing that the best part—the tender puck of impossibly sweet artichoke flesh—is still to come.

1. Break the stem off each artichoke; the stringiest fibers will come along with it. Remove any of the small outer leaves that seem tough. Rinse well.

2. Bring a large amount of salted water to a boil in a pot big enough to accommodate the artichokes in a single layer. Lower the artichokes into the boiling water, cover, and cook until the tip of a knife can be easily inserted into the stem end of the artichokes, 20 to 30 minutes, depending on the size.

3. Transfer the artichokes to a colander to drain upside down. Serve warm or cold, with the vinaigrette for dipping.

note The most under-celebrated aspect of eating an artichoke is the peculiar, faintly sweet flavor of the first sip of water you drink when you're done.

ARTICHOKES

The part of the artichoke plant we eat is the flower bud: it should feel firm and dense, its leaves tightly closed, smooth, and evenly colored. Keep in the refrigerator and use within two days of purchasing.

Leaves from
2 bunches of
radishes, turnips,
or beets (about
10 ounces / 280 g)

8 ounces / 225 g
dried short pasta,
such as fusilli or
orecchiette

Olive oil for cooking

3 medium / 150 g
shallots, finely diced

2 garlic cloves,
minced

Freshly grated
nutmeg

Fine sea salt

Extra-virgin olive oil

Freshly ground
black pepper

Aged Parmesan or
pecorino cheese,
shaved with a
vegetable peeler

12 walnut halves,
toasted (see page
68) and roughly
chopped

RADISH-TOP PASTA
Pâtes aux fanes de radis

When I buy radishes, I seek out the bunches with the prettiest leaves. The reason for this is twofold: it guarantees the radishes have been freshly picked, and it means I'll be able to eat the leaves themselves, a part of the plant that is often neglected. If I am to be perfectly honest, I must say I look forward to them even more than to the radishes themselves.

I use the leaves to make pesto and to fill miniature Corsican Turnovers with Winter Squash (page 119), but the quickest and most rewarding preparation is this pasta dish, which is ready in as much time as it takes to boil the pasta.

Use the leaves within a day or two of purchasing, as they will quickly go limp in the vegetable drawer.

1. Pick through the radish leaves and discard any that are wilted or discolored. Wash in cold water to remove all traces of sand or grit. Dry and chop roughly.

2. Bring salted water to a boil in a medium saucepan. Add the pasta and cook according to package directions until al dente.

3. While the pasta is cooking, heat a good swirl of cooking olive oil in a medium skillet over medium heat. Add the shallots and garlic. Cook, stirring often to avoid coloring, until softened, about 2 minutes.

4. Add the radish leaves to the skillet, sprinkle with a touch of nutmeg and some salt, stir, and let the leaves wilt briefly in the heat; they should become darker by a shade, but no more. Remove from the heat.

RECIPE CONTINUES

5. When the pasta is al dente, drain (not too thoroughly; keeping a little of the starchy cooking water makes the pasta silkier) and add to the skillet. Add a gurgle of extra-virgin olive oil and toss to combine over low heat. Sprinkle with pepper and divide between 2 warm pasta bowls or soup plates. Top with the cheese and walnuts and serve immediately.

RADISHES

The most common type of radish in France is pink-bottomed and white-shouldered, but you can use any color you prefer. It is more important to focus on finding small ones; their flavor is sweeter. Check that they feel firm, not limp or hollow, and that their leaves look pert and fresh—it is a sign they've been recently picked.

POOR MAN'S BOUILLABAISSE
Bouillabaisse du pauvre

From all of the many cookbooks my grandmother has given to me, our favorite is *La Véritable Cuisine provençale et niçoise*, which she bought when she lived in the South of France in the late thirties. The cooking of Provence is possibly the most produce-driven of all regional French cuisines and it has proven a precious source of inspiration in my vegetarian cooking.

The following dish was prompted by two different bouillabaisse recipes found in this book. When people think of bouillabaisse, they think of the most iconic example of the genre, a luxurious fish soup served with spicy mayonnaise. But it is also traditional to make a poor man's bouillabaisse, featuring fresh green peas for body and poached eggs for a silken mouthfeel—all in place of the seafood.

Beyond the fresh clean flavors of this soup, I love that it is served in two installments. First, you ladle the broth over a slice of bread and some spicy garlic mayonnaise; once that's been eaten, you serve the vegetables and poached egg with olive oil and lemon juice. The different elements can be prepared ahead, making this an elegant but low-stress dish to serve to guests.

1. Heat the cooking olive oil in a heavy-bottomed soup pot. Add the onion and garlic, sprinkle with ¼ teaspoon salt, and cook over medium heat, stirring often to avoid coloring, until softened, about 4 minutes. Add the fennel seeds and saffron and cook for a minute to awaken their flavor.

2. Add the potatoes and ¼ teaspoon salt. Pour in the white wine and stock. Cover, bring to a simmer, and cook for 8 minutes. Add the turnips, peas, and

RECIPE CONTINUES

1 tablespoon olive oil for cooking

1 small yellow onion (4¼ ounces / 120 g), finely chopped

2 garlic cloves, finely chopped

Fine sea salt

2 teaspoons fennel seeds

1 pinch saffron threads

12 ounces / 340 g new potatoes, scrubbed and halved

½ cup / 120 ml dry white wine

4 cups / 1 liter Vegetable Stock (page 198)

7 ounces / 200 g baby turnips, scrubbed

2 cups / 290 g shelled green peas, fresh or frozen

6 scallions (white and green parts), thinly sliced

4 slices country bread, toasted

Cheater's Spicy Garlic Mayonnaise (page 208)

4 Shell-Poached Eggs (page 215)

Extra-virgin olive oil

1 lemon, halved

Freshly ground black pepper

FRESH PEAS

When buying unshelled green peas, look for pods that are smooth and shiny; wrinkled or dull pods mean older, starchier peas. If you're not going to use the peas within a day or two of purchasing, shell and freeze them right away so they'll remain at their sweetest. You can then use them as you would fresh ones, without thawing. Note that 1 pound / 450 g unshelled pea pods will yield about 6 ounces / 170 g shelled peas.

scallions, and simmer until the potatoes are cooked through and the turnips and peas are firm-tender, 5 minutes. Taste and adjust the seasoning.

3. First, serve the broth. Tilt the pot to one side so the broth pools over the vegetables, and use a ladle to collect and transfer it to a heatproof pitcher; you should get about 4 cups / 1 liter. Keep the vegetables warm in the soup pot.

4. Spread the slices of bread with spicy garlic mayonnaise, cut them into fingers, and place at the bottom of 4 shallow soup bowls. Bring to the table and pour the broth into the bowls.

5. When the broth is eaten, divide the vegetables among the bowls. Break a poached egg into each, add a drizzle of extra-virgin olive oil and a squirt of lemon juice, sprinkle with pepper, and serve.

pantry gem

SAFFRON

Saffron is drawn from a flower, the saffron crocus (*Crocus sativus*). It comes in short, reddish-orange dried threads that turn dishes a rich shade of yellow and deliver a vibrant, one-of-a-kind flavor halfway between honey and hay. Saffron is water soluble, so it needs to be infused in a liquid component of your dish—which should be hot, acidic, or alcoholic—to unlock its full potential.

Saffron is a costly ingredient, but a small pinch is enough to set alight the flavors of a dish. Supermarket saffron typically lacks freshness and tastes dull; it is best to buy yours from a specialty spice store, whether online or in the real world. It's often more affordable to buy it by the ounce; perhaps you can place a group order with friends.

2 pounds / 900 g **young carrots**

1 tablespoon **olive oil** for cooking

1 small **red onion** (4¼ ounces / 120 g), minced

2 **garlic cloves**, finely chopped

Fine sea salt

1 medium **baking potato** (8 ounces / 225 g), peeled and diced

1 whole **star anise**

Seeds from 2 green **cardamom** pods or ¼ teaspoon ground green cardamom

1 small fresh **vanilla bean** or 2 teaspoons pure **vanilla** extract

4 cups / 1 liter **Vegetable Stock** (page 198)

1 tablespoon **sherry vinegar** or **cider vinegar**

2 cups / 480 ml plain unsweetened **almond milk**

2 tablespoons allnatural unsweetened **almond butter**

Freshly ground **black pepper**

Small bunch of **cilantro, flat-leaf parsley, chervil,** or **mint**

SOFTLY SPICED CARROT AND ALMOND SOUP

Velouté de carottes à l'amande et aux épices douces

In exploring a diet that relies on fewer animal products, I have found nondairy milks—plant milks derived from grains, legumes, seeds, or nuts—to be of particular interest. Each kind has its own flavor and consistency, so I like to buy and use them in a rotation. Although they present a different nutritional profile from cow's milk, they offer enough similarities that they can replace it in the kitchen, whether occasionally or regularly.

My preference goes to oat milk and almond milk: I use the former in crêpe batters and rice pudding, and I am very fond of the latter in this carrot soup, which can be served warm or chilled. Lightly spiced with star anise and vanilla, this soup rides on the subtle sweetness of the carrots and almond milk to form a delicate balance of flavors, and the result is both refined and satisfying. The flavors of this soup will deepen as it sits, so make it a day in advance if you can.

1. Peel the carrots or simply scrub them if they are thin-skinned and then slice into coins.

2. Heat the oil in a soup pot over medium heat. Add the onion and garlic, sprinkle with ½ teaspoon salt, and cook, stirring often to avoid coloring, until softened, about 4 minutes. Add the carrots, potato, star anise, and cardamom and sprinkle with ½ teaspoon salt. Cook, stirring from time to time, until the carrots are lightly golden, about 10 minutes.

RECIPE CONTINUES

3. Split the vanilla bean lengthwise with a sharp knife, scrape the seeds from the inside of the bean with the dull side of the blade, and add them and the bean to the pot. Add the stock and vinegar, cover, bring to a simmer, and cook until the vegetables are tender, about 15 minutes.

4. Remove from the heat, fish out the vanilla bean and star anise (save them for another use), and add the almond milk. Use a blender or an immersion blender to purée the soup until smooth. You can make the recipe a day in advance up to this point: Add the vanilla and star anise back in so they'll continue to infuse in the soup, then cool completely, cover, and refrigerate.

5. When ready to serve, mix the almond butter with 1 tablespoon cold water in a small bowl to get a smooth and pourable consistency.

6. Reheat the soup without allowing it to boil. Taste and adjust the seasoning. Serve topped with the thinned almond butter, freshly ground pepper, and a few sprigs of cilantro.

SWISS CHARD PIE WITH PRUNES AND PINE NUTS

Tourte aux blettes, pruneaux et pignons

SERVES 4

7 ounces / 200 g
Swiss chard leaves,
from 4 large or
6 small stalks

8 medium prunes,
pitted

3 medium / 150 g
shallots

2 garlic cloves

1 tablespoon olive oil
for cooking

Fine sea salt

Spelt Tart Dough
(page 205) or
1 pound frozen puff
pastry, thawed

2 tablespoons
rolled spelt or oats

3 tablespoons
pine nuts, toasted
(see page 68)

Freshly ground
black pepper

1 large organic
egg yolk

One of my mother's spring staples is a savory pie made with two layers of puff pastry filled with Swiss chard leaves, a handful of raisins, and a scattering of pine nuts. In my kitchen, it has morphed into this recipe, assembled on a yeast-raised dough made with spelt flour and garnished with chopped prunes.

Most Swiss chard tart or pie recipes have you cook the leaves before assembling the dish, but this causes them to overcook and lose their vibrancy. I prefer my mother's unconventional technique of piling the raw leaves in the center of the pie before topping them with a second circle of dough. The giant pile feels a little precarious at first, but the leaves cook down in the oven and the top crust will follow.

This pie is equally good hot or at room temperature, served with a salad of mixed greens, and you can pack slices for a picnic or lunch at the office, as they are easily eaten out of hand. This recipe makes use of the leaf part of the Swiss chard only. Chop the stalks and add to a stir-fry or a risotto or use them to make Pickled Swiss Chard Stalks (page 43).

1. Preheat the oven to 400°F. / 200°C.

2. Rinse the Swiss chard leaves and dry in a salad spinner. Chop into strips.

3. In a food processor, chop the prunes, shallots, garlic, oil, and ½ teaspoon salt until they form a paste. (Alternatively, chop finely by hand.)

RECIPE CONTINUES

4. Divide the dough in half. Dust one piece of dough with a little flour and roll it out on a sheet of parchment paper into an 11-inch / 28 cm circle. Transfer to a baking sheet.

5. Spread the prune mixture gently over the circle of dough, leaving a 1-inch / 2.5 cm border all around; there won't be enough of the mixture to cover the dough, just make sure it's evenly spread out. Sprinkle the rolled spelt on top; it will absorb excess moisture and prevent the bottom crust from getting soggy.

6. Add the pine nuts and arrange the chopped chard on top, without letting it fall onto the clear border. It will look like a very large pile at this stage; this is normal. Grind some pepper over the chard.

7. In a small bowl, whisk together the egg yolk and 1 tablespoon cold water; use some of this to moisten the edges of the dough. Reserve the remaining egg yolk mixture.

8. Dust the second piece of dough with a little flour and roll it out on a lightly floured surface into a 12-inch / 30 cm circle. Drape it over the pile of chard, making sure the edges line up with the bottom crust. Crimp with a fork to seal the edges and nick the top in a few places with the tip of your knife to make steam vents.

9. Brush the top crust with the reserved egg yolk mixture and bake until golden brown, about 25 minutes. Cut into slices with a serrated bread knife.

pantry gem

PRUNES

Ah, prunes. It saddens me greatly that this extraordinary dried fruit gets such a bad rap in North America. We French love our *pruneaux* and when we're not simply snacking on them, with a few almonds or a square of dark chocolate, we use them in savory dishes and desserts with equal enthusiasm. Before you fall back on the preconceived notion that prunes—or dried plums, as they are marketed nowadays—are no more than a digestive aid, do seek out good, plump, freshly dried prunes. Taste them and see for yourself how sweet, fruity, and aromatic they are.

SERVES 4

1 cup / 130 g
all-purpose flour

Fine sea salt

4 large organic
eggs, 2 whole
and 2 separated

Freshly ground
black pepper

1 garlic clove,
finely chopped

2 tablespoons dry
white wine (optional)

½ cup / 120 ml
milk (not skim) or
unflavored,
unsweetened
nondairy milk

8 ounces / 225 g
Swiss chard leaves
(save the stalks for
another use) or
spinach, finely
chopped

Olive oil for cooking

GREEN PANCAKES
Pascadous

I stumbled upon this dish the year my boyfriend, Maxence, and
I drove across the Aveyron, a mountainous and starkly gorgeous
region in the heart of France. We stopped in the village of
Laguiole, wanting to buy some of the famous artisanal knives,
with the signature bee on the handle, that are produced there—
and shamelessly counterfeited around the world.

Having parted with a good lump of money for a beautiful set
of handmade dinner knives, we found our way into a bustling
little restaurant across from the town hall and proceeded to
order lunch. I asked about the *pascadous* listed on the menu and
was told they are small pancakes made with sliced Swiss chard
leaves. My curiosity was rewarded when the plate appeared and
I took a bite from one of the golden, lightly crusty rounds, fluffy
and richly green inside.

I make these often now, with Swiss chard or spinach, and,
if I have it, I add sorrel, too, for a nice tang. They make for a
lovely weeknight dinner, paired with a green salad, and they're
a welcome brunch item, too.

1. In a medium bowl, combine the flour and 1 teaspoon
   salt and form a well in the center. Add 2 whole eggs
   and 2 egg yolks and stir to mix with part of the flour
   from the mound. Sprinkle with pepper. Add the garlic
   and wine and then pour the milk in a slow stream,
   whisking as you go, until all the flour is incorporated
   and the mixture is creamy and mostly lump-free.
   Cover and refrigerate for at least 2 hours, or overnight.

2. When ready to cook the pancakes, remove the bowl
   from the fridge and fold in the greens.

3. In a clean bowl, beat the 2 egg whites with ¼ teaspoon salt with a handheld electric mixer or a whisk until they form stiff peaks. Fold them into the batter with a spatula, working in a circular, up-and-down motion to avoid deflating the egg whites.

4. Heat 1 tablespoon cooking olive oil in a large skillet over medium heat. Ladle about ¼ cup / 60 ml of the batter into the hot skillet, without flattening. Repeat to form as many pancakes as will comfortably fit in the skillet, probably no more than 4.

5. Cook until the edges are set and the pancakes are golden underneath, 4 to 5 minutes. Flip and cook until the other side is set and golden, 3 to 4 minutes. Transfer to a warmed serving plate, grease the skillet again, and repeat with the remaining batter. You should have enough to make 10 to 12 pancakes.

6. Serve hot, adding a little more pepper and a sprinkling of salt on top.

Olive oil **for cooking**

1 small yellow onion (4¼ ounces / 120 g), thinly sliced

Fine sea salt

Freshly grated nutmeg

3 scallions (white and green parts), thinly sliced

1¼ pounds / 560 g green asparagus, preferably thin ones

Extra-virgin olive oil

Buckwheat Yogurt Tart Dough (page 199)

Zest of 1 organic lemon, cut into thin strips

Freshly ground black pepper

ASPARAGUS BUCKWHEAT TART
Tarte asperge et sarrasin

You and I might think we're pretty passionate about asparagus, but we have nothing on the Germans: they really do love their asparagus and celebrate the season with as much abandon as, say, Americans on Halloween or the Japanese in cherry blossom season. Shop windows are redecorated to match the theme, entire dinner parties are thrown in honor of the green stalk, and eager cooks buy just about every gadget imaginable to peel, prepare, and serve it.

It's about more than the vegetable, of course; it's about welcoming the first sprightly thing to pop out of the earth after a long winter of turnips and potatoes. As someone who greets any change of season with excitement, I can get behind that idea.

The most common way to eat asparagus, in Germany as in France, is to pick up each stalk with your fingers, dip it in vinaigrette, and munch your way down, bite after bite. I do enjoy serving them in this manner, but I also like to use them to garnish savory tarts. This square one features a variation on my yogurt-based tart crust, made here with buckwheat flour; the subtle malted notes complement the asparagus beautifully.

1. Heat a glug of cooking olive oil in a skillet over medium heat. Add the onion, sprinkle with ¼ teaspoon salt and a touch of nutmeg, and stir to combine. Cover, reduce the heat, and cook, stirring from time to time, until very soft, about 20 minutes. Add the scallions and cook for another 5 minutes. Taste, adjust the seasoning, and remove from the heat.

2. Trim the bottom of the asparagus stalks, just to remove the woody part. Using a mandoline slicer

or sharp vegetable peeler, shave 4 of the asparagus
stalks lengthwise into long ribbons, as thin as you can,
and put these in a medium bowl. Add a thin drizzle
of extra-virgin olive oil and a pinch of salt and toss
to coat.

3. Prepare the rest of the asparagus for roasting: If the
   stalks are thick, halve or quarter them lengthwise.
   Place in a baking dish, drizzle with a little cooking
   olive oil, sprinkle with ½ teaspoon salt, and roll side to
   side to coat.

4. Preheat the oven to 400°F. / 200°C.

5. Roll out the dough between two sheets of parchment
   paper to form a 12-inch / 30 cm square. Remove the
   top sheet of paper and roll the edges of the dough over

RECIPE CONTINUES

themselves to form a small ridge all around, pressing down as you go. Transfer the dough on the parchment paper to a baking sheet. Prick all over with a fork, cover with the top piece of parchment, and top with baking weights.

6. Place both the baking dish of asparagus and the baking sheet of dough in the oven to bake until the asparagus is roasted and the crust is golden brown, about 30 minutes.

7. Remove the top sheet of parchment and baking weights (be careful; they will be hot) from the crust. Spread the onion mixture over the crust and arrange the roasted asparagus on top, lining them up and arranging them so that the tips alternate which side they point to. Arrange the raw asparagus ribbons in loops on top, sprinkle with the strips of lemon zest and black pepper, and cut square servings with a serrated knife.

ASPARAGUS

Look for firm and smooth stalks that stand upright, with tips that look like tightly closed buds, and a color that's vibrant rather than dull. The cut ends shouldn't look overly dry. I prefer thin asparagus to fat ones, but more important than their actual girth is that the bunch you pick be of comparable thickness, so they'll cook evenly.

After purchase, remove the band that holds the bunch together and plop the asparagus like a bouquet into a wide-mouthed jar. Add a little water to the bottom, cover loosely with a plastic bag, and keep in the fridge for a day or two.

PICKLED SWISS CHARD STALKS
Tiges de blettes en aigre-doux

MAKES 2 CUPS /
480 ML

**7 ounces / 200 g
Swiss chard stalks,
preferably from
young multicolored
plants**

**½ cup / 120 ml
cider vinegar**

**2 tablespoons
unrefined blond
cane sugar (also
sold as evaporated
cane juice)**

**2 teaspoons
fine sea salt**

**1 teaspoon
coriander seeds**

**1 teaspoon
fennel seeds**

My grandmother used to make her own cornichons, the tiny gherkins pickled in white wine vinegar with pearl onions, tarragon, and coriander seeds. It is a labor-intensive process that involves rubbing the gherkins to rid them of their downy fuzz, macerating them in salt to drain out most of their juice, and patting them dry, lovingly, one by one. Then you have to pack the tiny cucumbers in vinegar, boil the jars, and let them ripen for months.

Much better suited to my impatient nature is quick-pickling: simply boiling vinegar with water, sugar, and salt and pouring that hot mixture over any crisp vegetable. I was once inspired to quick-pickle the thin stalks of a bunch of Swiss chard I'd bought to make a Swiss Chard Pie with Prunes and Pine Nuts (page 35). The multicolored stalks looked so pretty, in hues of pink, yellow, red, and cream, that putting them in a jar to hold onto seemed the way to go.

The resulting *aigre-doux*—the French term for pickle, combining the words for sour and sweet—is ready to eat within a couple of days and works wonders in a sandwich or an omelet, on a salad or a bowl of noodles, or as a snack, with a piece of hard cheese and a slice of crusty bread.

1. Have ready a clean 2-cup / 480 ml canning jar with a tight-fitting lid.

2. If the Swiss chard stalks are wide, cut them into two or three lengthwise strips. Slice crosswise into ⅓-inch / 8 mm pieces and pack them into the jar.

3. In a small saucepan, combine the vinegar, sugar, salt, coriander seeds, fennel seeds, and 1 cup / 240 ml

RECIPE CONTINUES

water. Set over medium-high heat, stir until the sugar and salt are dissolved, and bring to a boil. (The smell of boiling vinegar is quite pungent. If you're expecting guests or potential buyers for your house, avoid making this just before they arrive.)

4. As soon as the mixture boils, remove from the heat and pour into the jar. Close the lid tightly (the jar will be very hot) and let cool to room temperature before refrigerating.

5. The pickle will be ready to eat by the next day, but the flavor will be optimal after 2 to 3 days. Keep in the fridge for up to a month.

BRETON SHORTBREAD COOKIES (OR TART DOUGH)

Sablés bretons (ou pâte sablé breton)

MAKES 12 COOKIES OR ONE 10- TO 12-INCH / 25 TO 30 CM TART CRUST

⅓ cup / 70 g unrefined blond cane **sugar** (also sold as evaporated cane juice)

6 tablespoons / 85 g high-quality unsalted **butter**, softened

1 small fresh **vanilla bean** or 2 teaspoons pure **vanilla** extract

1 large organic **egg**

1 cup / 130 g all-purpose **flour**

1 teaspoon **baking powder**

½ teaspoon **fine sea salt**

The type of cookies you eat after school as a child informs your taste buds for life. When I was growing up, a family standby was the *palet breton*, a shortbread cookie from Brittany. Buttery, crisp, and dangerously crumb-prone, they had to be eaten over a plate held close to our chins, propped against the graphic novels we read avidly, cross-legged on the couch. I found out years later how simple they are to make at home, and it gives me great satisfaction every time I do, biting into one as soon as it cools and relishing the sensation of the cookie shattering into a thousand little crumbs on my tongue.

This is a two-in-one recipe that can be used to make cut-out cookies, like the ones I grew up eating, or baked into a thick crust for a fruit tart. In that case, you'll either bake the crust first and then garnish it with fresh fruit, as for the Strawberry Tartlets (page 48), or bake the fruit directly on top, as for the Easy Fresh Fig Tart (page 138).

1. In the bowl of a stand mixer fitted with the paddle attachment, combine the sugar and butter. (Alternatively, do this by hand in a bowl with a wooden spoon.) Split the vanilla bean lengthwise with a sharp knife, scrape the seeds from the inside of the bean with the dull side of the blade, and add them to the sugar and butter. Beat the sugar and butter at low speed until pale and fluffy, about 3 minutes. Add the egg and beat for 2 minutes.

RECIPE CONTINUES

2. In another bowl, combine the flour, baking powder, and salt, stirring with a whisk to remove any lumps. Add to the mixer and mix at low speed for a few seconds, just until no trace of flour remains. The dough will be quite soft.

TO MAKE SHORTBREAD COOKIES

Transfer the dough to a container and refrigerate for at least 2 hours, and preferably overnight.

Preheat the oven to 350°F. / 175°C. and line a baking sheet with parchment paper or a silicone baking mat.

Remove the dough from the fridge and roll it out between two sheets of parchment paper to a thickness of ⅓ inch / 8 mm. Peel off the top sheet gently and use a round cookie cutter, about 2 inches / 5 cm in diameter, to cut out circles of dough. Transfer to the prepared baking sheet, giving them a little room to expand.

Gather the scraps of dough and repeat to cut out more cookies. As the dough warms to room temperature, it may become too soft to work with; place it in the freezer for 10 minutes to firm up before cutting out circles again.

Bake the sablés until golden brown, 15 to 20 minutes. Transfer to a rack to cool completely. The sablés will keep for a few days in an airtight container at room temperature.

pantry gem

FRESH VANILLA BEANS

I used to avoid baking with fresh vanilla beans because they seemed pricey and hardly worth the trouble in terms of flavor, but that was because I had only ever known the gnarly old beans that most supermarkets sell for the price of gold. Then I started ordering them online, directly from a Tahitian producer, and although they're still not cheap, these vanilla beans are so fat, fresh, and oozing with flavor that they're worth every penny.

Transfer the dough to an ungreased 10- to 12-inch / 25 to 30 cm round cake or tart pan with a removable bottom. Alternatively, arrange eight 3-inch / 8 cm pastry rings (see below) on a baking sheet lined with parchment paper or a silicone baking mat and divide the dough evenly among them. Press the dough into an even layer with a flexible spatula or the tips of your moistened fingers. Cover loosely with plastic wrap and refrigerate for at least 2 hours, and preferably overnight.

Preheat the oven to 350°F. / 175°C.

Bake until golden brown, 35 minutes for a single tart, 25 minutes for tartlets. Transfer to a rack to cool for 20 minutes before loosening and cautiously removing the sides of the tart pan or pastry rings. Let cool completely before topping. The crust may be prepared a few hours ahead; once cool, cover loosely with a clean kitchen towel.

ABOUT PASTRY RINGS

A pastry ring is a ring made of stainless steel—imagine a cake pan with no bottom—that comes in different diameters, but is typically 2 inches / 5 cm in height. It is used by pastry chefs and serious home bakers to create cakes, tarts, and mousses with neat, straight sides.

MAKES EIGHT
3-INCH / 8 CM
TARTLETS,
OR ONE 10- TO
12-INCH / 25
TO 30 CM TART

Lemon Pastry Cream (page 217)

Breton Shortbread Tart Dough (page 45), baked

1¼ pounds / 560 g strawberries, preferably small, hulled and halved or quartered depending on their size

2 tablespoons strawberry jam (optional)

STRAWBERRY TARTLETS WITH BRETON SHORTBREAD CRUST

Tartelettes aux fraises, sablé breton

When strawberries come into season in the spring, I go through an initial period of wanting nothing more than to eat them plain, simply holding them by the ruffle of their tiny leaves and biting off the ruby flesh, to enjoy their juicy sweetness with no distraction. Once that phase is over, I get itchy for the most glorious dessert in the world: a strawberry tart. These tartlets, which emulate a popular style found in Paris pâtisseries, feature a thick Breton shortbread crust that crumbles in the mouth and a light pastry cream flavored with lemon.

1. Spoon the pastry cream onto the crust(s) and spread into an even layer. Arrange the strawberries over the cream in a circular pattern, starting from the center.

2. If desired, prepare a jam glaze to give the tartlets more shine: In a small saucepan, heat the jam with 1 tablespoon water until syrupy, without allowing it to boil. If the jam contains bits of fruit, strain it. Glaze the strawberries lightly with the syrup using a pastry brush. Let set for 10 minutes before serving.

STRAWBERRIES

Pick strawberries that are bright and evenly colored; turn up your nose at underripe ones that are white near the stem. A nose-tickling strawberry smell is a good indication that the flavor won't disappoint.

9 ounces / 250 g good-quality bittersweet chocolate (about 65% cacao)

6 extra-large organic egg whites

½ teaspoon cream of tartar

½ teaspoon fine sea salt

3 tablespoons / 35 g unrefined blond cane sugar (also sold as evaporated cane juice)

⅓ cup / 40 g cacao nibs (optional)

DARK CHOCOLATE MOUSSE, THREE WAYS

Mousse au chocolat noir de trois façons

I've always been an ardent lover of chocolate mousse and I've tinkered with many recipes over the years, but the one I return to again and again is this pared-down formula that uses just chocolate, egg whites, and a little sugar—no cream, no egg yolks. Intensely chocolaty and almost truffle-like in texture, it is a purist's chocolate mousse; a small serving is enough to satisfy.

Its beauty also lies in its versatility: the same mixture can be frozen to make sorbet without an ice cream machine, or baked in ramekins to make molten chocolate cakes.

1. Melt the chocolate (see page 51), transfer to a medium bowl, and set aside to cool.

2. In the bowl of a stand mixer fitted with the whisk attachment (or in a clean bowl using a handheld electric mixer), combine the egg whites, cream of tartar, and salt. Beat the egg whites on medium speed until they are frothy throughout, about 3 minutes. Add the sugar and beat on medium-high speed until they form stiff, glossy peaks.

3. Stir about one-sixth of the egg whites into the melted chocolate. Add another sixth of the egg whites and this time fold them in with a spatula, lifting the mixture from the center out and turning the bowl every time, until fully incorporated. Continue adding the rest of the egg whites in four additions, until they have all been incorporated. Halfway through, fold in the cacao nibs (if using).

TO MAKE CHOCOLATE MOUSSE

Pour the mixture into one 3-cup / 720 ml bowl or six ½-cup / 120 ml ramekins or glasses. Cover and refrigerate until set, at least 4 hours, and preferably overnight.

TO MAKE MOLTEN CHOCOLATE CAKES

Grease six ½-cup / 120 ml ovenproof ramekins and divide the chocolate mousse mixture among them. Cover and reserve in the fridge until ready to bake.

Preheat the oven to 350°F. / 175°C.

Bake the ramekins until the tops are set and cracked, about 12 minutes. Transfer to a rack and let rest for 5 to 10 minutes before serving directly in the ramekins (warn your guests that they will still be hot). The sides should be cake-like and the centers custardy.

TO MAKE CHOCOLATE SORBET

Pour the chocolate mousse into a freezer container with a tight-fitting lid. Refrigerate until completely cold and then transfer to the freezer for a few hours or overnight, until frozen.

note Because the egg whites in the mousse and sorbet are not cooked, use the freshest eggs you can find. Even so, pregnant women, young children, and people with a weakened immune system shouldn't eat preparations containing raw eggs.

MELTING CHOCOLATE

Chocolate doesn't like direct, strong heat, and the best method for melting it is in a double boiler. It is easy to improvise with a saucepan filled with an inch of water, and a heatproof bowl set over (but not touching) the simmering water. Stir the chocolate often to ensure even melting.

POACHED RHUBARB AND ORANGE SALAD

Salade de rhubarbe pochée et orange

SERVES 4

1 pound / 450 g rhubarb

⅔ cup / 140 g unrefined blond cane sugar (also sold as evaporated cane juice)

1 small fresh vanilla bean or 2 teaspoons pure vanilla extract

4 small oranges

Gazelle Horn Sorbet (page 55)

½ cup / 70 g whole almonds, toasted (see page 68) and roughly chopped

The Paris dining scene is rife with pocket-size restaurants owned by independent chefs who can't afford anything larger but whose talents shine in such intimate, funky settings. Among these "micro-gastros" is one called Rino, run by Giovanni Passerini, a Roman chef who came to Paris seeking creative freedom and an appreciative audience. That he certainly found, and diners line up to fill his twenty seats, eager for a taste of his luminous, market-driven dishes.

This dessert is inspired by one he served on an April night: a rhubarb and orange salad—the rhubarb lightly poached, the orange segments peeled—topped with a handful of mixed nuts. It was a remarkably light and aromatic dessert that I immediately reproduced in my own kitchen, taking advantage of that precious time in the spring when rhubarb has arrived and oranges haven't yet departed. I like to serve it with a smooth and creamy almond sorbet spiked with orange flower water.

1. Cut the rhubarb stalks in ⅓-inch / 8 mm slices, unless they are pencil-thin, in which case you should cut them in 1-inch / 2.5 cm segments.

2. In a medium saucepan, combine the sugar and 2 cups / 480 ml water. Split the vanilla bean lengthwise with a sharp knife, scrape the seeds from the inside of the bean with the dull side of the blade, and add them and the bean to the pan. Bring to a simmer, stirring often as the sugar dissolves.

RECIPE CONTINUES

3. Add half of the rhubarb to the simmering syrup, cover, and allow the mixture to return to a simmer. Once it simmers, cook for just 1 minute, until the rhubarb pieces are tender—test them with the tip of a knife; it should meet minimal resistance—but still holding their shape. Remove the rhubarb with a slotted spoon and transfer to a container. Repeat with the rest of the rhubarb and add it along with the syrup and vanilla bean (it will continue to impart its flavor) to the container. Let cool to room temperature, cover, and refrigerate until chilled. This can be prepared a day ahead. Remove from the refrigerator 30 minutes before serving.

4. Segment the oranges (see page 160) and divide among 4 dessert bowls. Spoon the rhubarb on top so the amount of rhubarb and orange segments is about the same, and add 2 or 3 tablespoons of the rhubarb syrup to each bowl.

5. Add a scoop of sorbet, sprinkle with the almonds, and serve.

note Use the leftover rhubarb syrup to make cocktails with sparkling white wine or seltzer.

GAZELLE HORN SORBET
Sorbet corne de gazelle

MAKES 2 CUPS /
480 ML

½ cup / 120 g
smooth all-natural
unsweetened
almond butter,
chilled

⅓ cup / 70 g
unrefined blond
cane sugar (also
sold as evaporated
cane juice)

1 teaspoon orange
flower water, or
more to taste

1¼ cups / 300 ml
sparkling water,
chilled

When I was growing up, my family often went out to eat at a Moroccan restaurant around the corner from our apartment. After the couscous dishes were cleared, the waiter would appear with a silver tray the size of a satellite dish bearing a full selection of picture-perfect North African pastries in pastel colors. We were allowed one each, and I usually went for the gazelle horn, a thin, crescent-shaped shell filled with almond paste flavored with orange flower water.

This heavenly taste memory prompted me to add a dash of orange flower water the day I tried turning almond butter into a sorbet. The almond butter makes it smooth and creamy and the sparkling water makes the mixture slightly foamy before you churn it, helping to make the sorbet fluffier. A scoop of it makes a nice garnish for fruit salads or soups—such as Poached Rhubarb and Orange Salad (page 52) or Melon and Ginger Soup (page 102)—or it can be frozen in ice pop molds for a lickable treat.

1. In a medium bowl, stir together the almond butter, sugar, and orange flower water. Pour in the sparkling water slowly, whisking constantly to incorporate it into the almond butter. The mixture will be frothy. Taste and add a little more orange flower water, if desired; the amount you'll need depends on your taste and the potency of your orange flower water.

2. Freeze in an ice cream maker according to the manufacturer's instructions. Serve immediately or freeze for later; 20 minutes before serving, put the frozen sorbet in the fridge to soften slightly.

MAKES 2 DOZEN

1¼ cups / 200 g fine-grind stone-ground cornmeal

6 tablespoons / 50 g all-purpose flour

¼ teaspoon baking soda

¼ teaspoon fine sea salt

Zest of 1 organic lemon, zested into fine strips (see Note)

½ cup / 100 g unrefined blond cane sugar (also sold as evaporated cane juice)

8 tablespoons / 120 g high-quality unsalted butter, softened

2 large organic eggs

¼ cup / 60 ml freshly squeezed lemon juice

LEMON CORN COOKIES
Jembelles

I first heard about *jembelles* while leafing through a fascinating cookbook called *La Cuisine paysanne de Savoie* by Marie-Thérèse Hermann, who gathered nineteenth-century recipes that document the peasant cuisine of Savoy, a mountainous region in the southeast of France. Jembelles are simple cookies made with cornmeal (in Savoyard it is called polenta, a word borrowed from nearby Piedmont; the final "a" is silent) and flavored with lemon zest.

I tinkered with the recipe to tone the sugar down a bit and dial up the lemon flavor and settled on this version, which produces moist little cookies, slightly gritty from the cornmeal and robustly lemony from the use of both the juice and zest of the fruit. Make sure you use a fine-grind cornmeal here; a coarse one won't get you the right texture. Other citruses can replace the lemon; lime and orange make pleasing variations.

1. Preheat the oven to 400°F. / 200°C. and line a baking sheet with parchment paper or a silicone baking mat.

2. In a medium bowl, combine the cornmeal, flour, baking soda, salt, and lemon zest, stirring with a whisk to remove any lumps.

3. In the bowl of a stand mixer fitted with the paddle attachment, beat the sugar and butter until creamy, about 2 minutes. (Alternatively, do this by hand in a bowl with a wooden spoon.) Beat in the eggs and lemon juice; the mixture will look curdled. Add the dry ingredients and stir until just combined.

4. Drop tablespoonfuls of the batter onto the prepared baking sheet, leaving 2 inches / 5 cm of space between them.

5. Bake until the cookies are set and the edges are golden brown, about 15 minutes. Transfer to a rack to cool completely. The cookies will keep for a few days in an airtight container at room temperature.

note To make thin strips of lemon zest for these cookies, I use a zester that has four sharp little holes that you scrape against the skin of the lemon, almost as if you were combing it. A Microplane zester can be used, too, but preferably the coarse kind. If you have neither of those tools, peel off wide strips of the lemon zest with a vegetable peeler, taking care not to get too much of the white pith, and use a sharp knife to slice them into the thinnest slivers you can.

SUMMER

L'été

French summers are officially launched with the Fête de la Musique, a national festival that encourages musicians to come out and play on the street. It's also an invitation to find a patch of green and have a picnic, as Parisians do at the first hint of mild weather, setting up camp on the nearest park lawn or by one of the canals.

In summer, I find myself gravitating toward the cuisines of Provence, the French Basque country, or Corsica, which make the most enthusiastic use of sun-kissed produce. The dishes in this chapter offer options to make both quick, simple meals for when your appetite has melted in the heat as well as more sophisticated preparations to please a tableful of friends.

PRODUCE TO PLAY WITH IN THE SUMMER

- Apricots
- Artichokes
- Beets
- Bell peppers
- Black currants
- Blueberries
- Broccoli

- Celery
- Cherries
- Cucumbers
- Eggplants
- Fennel
- Figs
- Garlic

- Green beans
- Kohlrabi
- Lettuce and other salad greens
- Melon
- Nectarines

- Onions
- Peaches
- Potatoes
- Raspberries
- Red currants
- Rhubarb

- Shell beans
- Swiss chard
- Tomatoes
- Watermelon
- Zucchini and other summer squash

**2 pounds / 900 g
small eggplants**

**2 garlic cloves,
cut into thin slivers**

**12 brine-cured
black olives, such
as Kalamata, pitted**

**2 tablespoons
freshly squeezed
lemon juice**

**1 tablespoon extra-
virgin olive oil**

**1 cup / 20 g chopped
fresh flat-leaf parsley
leaves**

Fine sea salt

**Freshly ground
black pepper**

Hot sauce

EGGPLANT AND
BLACK OLIVE CAVIAR

Caviar d'aubergine aux olives noires

When I come home from the market with eggplants in my
basket, eggplant "caviar" is what I am most eager to make.
Roasting is a foolproof method for cooking eggplants, and then
it's just a matter of puréeing the flesh to produce a marvelously
silky spread to serve with slices of baguette or pita triangles at
the cocktail hour or for a picnic spread. Eggplant caviar can also
be used in sandwiches or scooped over a bowl of rice.

I have made countless versions of this Provençal classic over
the years, experimenting with whatever flavoring ingredients
waved at me from the shelves of my pantry, but this is the one
I like best. It gets a good tang from black olives and refreshing
notes from the lemon and parsley.

1. Roast the eggplants a few hours in advance or the day
   before. Use a knife to pierce three or four slits in each
   eggplant and slip the garlic slivers into the slits.

2. Place the whole eggplants on a lightly oiled baking
   sheet and insert in the cold oven. Turn the oven to
   400°F. / 200°C. and roast the eggplants, flipping them
   halfway through, until completely soft, 45 minutes to
   1 hour. Set aside to cool completely. If roasting the day
   before, put the eggplants in an airtight container and
   refrigerate.

3. Halve the eggplants lengthwise and scoop out the flesh
   and garlic cloves with a tablespoon, scraping the skin
   to get as much flesh as possible. It's okay if a little of

the skin comes with it. Put the eggplant and garlic in a food processor or blender.

4. Add the olives, lemon juice, olive oil, parsley, a pinch of salt, a good grind of black pepper, and a dash of hot sauce. Process until very smooth (or chop the mixture by hand as finely as possible). Taste and adjust the seasoning.

EGGPLANTS

Younger, smaller eggplants are definitely preferable; they taste sweeter, with no hint of bitterness. Regardless of the size, pick eggplants that feel heavy, have a smooth and shiny skin, and a stem-end "hat" that looks green and fresh.

GOAT CHEESE AND ROSEMARY SABLÉS

Sablés au chèvre et au romarin

MAKES 4 DOZEN
SABLÉS

8 ounces / 225 g
fresh **goat cheese**

2 tablespoons finely
chopped fresh
rosemary or
1 tablespoon dried

2 teaspoons
fine sea salt

1 teaspoon **honey**

½ teaspoon freshly
ground **black pepper**

¼ cup / 60 ml
extra-virgin olive oil

2 large organic
egg yolks

1½ cups / 195 g
all-purpose flour,
or more if needed

When I was a child and our parents had dinner guests, my sister and I would feel tremendous excitement at the prospect of being allowed to sit on the carpet by the coffee table and devour the pretzel sticks, roasted peanuts, and tiny cheese crackers that normally lived in a special box high up in the kitchen cabinet above the sink.

Now that I am all grown up, I hardly ever buy anything like this from the store; home-baked apéritif nibbles turn out to be easy to make and I love that I have control over just what goes into them, unlike with store-bought, which are often loaded with additives. I also have to admit to deriving an absurd amount of gratification from making these for friends, who invariably ask, their mouths full, "Wow, you really made those yourself?"

I like to make bite-size savory cookies, flavored with goat cheese and rosemary, using the slice-and-bake method so I can have a batch in the oven in no time. The dough can be prepared in advance and kept in the freezer, ready to be sliced and baked for an apéritif spread or served with a green salad.

1. In a medium bowl, mash the goat cheese with the rosemary, salt, honey, pepper, olive oil, and egg yolks until smooth.

2. Stir in the flour. When most of it is absorbed, turn out the mixture onto a clean work surface and knead gently until it comes together into a smooth ball of dough. Add a little more flour if needed.

RECIPE CONTINUES

3. Divide into 4 equal pieces and roll each into a log about 1 inch / 2.5 cm in diameter. Wrap in plastic or parchment paper and place in the freezer for 1 hour. (If you prepare the dough further in advance, wrap the logs tightly to avoid freezer burn and transfer to the fridge 1 hour before slicing.)

4. Preheat the oven to 350°F. / 175°C. and line a baking sheet with parchment paper or a silicone baking mat.

5. Take one log out of the freezer and cut it into ½-inch / 1 cm slices. Arrange on the prepared baking sheet, leaving a little space between them. Repeat with the remaining dough, working in batches.

6. Bake until golden, 15 to 20 minutes. Transfer to a rack to cool completely. The texture of these is most enjoyable on the day they're baked, but they will keep for a few days in an airtight container at room temperature.

SHAVED FENNEL SALAD WITH PRESERVED LEMON

Salade de fenouil cru au citron confit

SERVES 4

4 medium / 1 kg fennel bulbs

3 tablespoons diced **Preserved Lemons** (page 89)

Honey Lemon Vinaigrette (page 207), made without the salt

Freshly ground black pepper

Because of my childhood aversion to aniseed, it has taken me years to develop an appreciation for raw fennel. The turning point for me has been to discover that, when thinly sliced, it becomes a completely different animal, and that feathery wisps of raw fennel make for the most aromatic of salads.

I add fennel shavings to what the French call *salades composées*, or multi-ingredient salads, for complexity and crunch. But it plays an incredible solo, too, with background support from preserved lemon—an enchanting condiment drawn from the cuisine of Morocco—and a sweet-and-sour vinaigrette.

This makes a good salad for a picnic or packed lunch, as the flavors will develop as it sits. And if fennel isn't your thing, this salad can be made with small waxy potatoes, steamed and halved, in its place.

1. Trim the fennel stalks and save them for your stock box (see page 198), keeping a few fennel fronds for garnish. Slice off the root end. Using a mandoline slicer or very sharp knife, cut the fennel into the thinnest shavings you can.

2. Put the fennel in a medium salad bowl and add the diced preserved lemon and honey lemon vinaigrette. Sprinkle with black pepper and add a few fennel fronds. Toss to coat and serve.

SERVES 6

**2 pounds / 900 g
haricots verts or
thin green beans,
trimmed**

**3 tablespoons
all-natural
unsweetened
almond butter**

**3 tablespoons
extra-virgin olive oil**

**3 tablespoons
freshly squeezed
lemon juice**

**1 tablespoon
cider vinegar**

**1 teaspoon fine
sea salt**

**3 cups / 450 g
cooked red rice or
brown rice, cooled
(from about 1 cup /
200 g uncooked rice)**

**⅔ cup / 85 g
almonds, toasted
(see page 68) and
roughly chopped**

**1 cup / 20 g chopped
fresh flat-leaf parsley
leaves**

**Freshly ground
black pepper**

GREEN BEAN, RED RICE, AND ALMOND SALAD

Salade de haricots verts, riz rouge et amandes

Always on the lookout for tasty tricks for using leftover rice, I came up with this salad early one summer when I had a bag of the first haricots verts of the season, which I wanted to cook before they lost their youthful bounce, and a tub of cooked red rice from the night before. The result was this flavorsome salad, which has since become a fixture in my summer rotation.

Red rice is a whole, or partially hulled, rice whose outer husk is dark red rather than the more common brown. It is very nutritious and I enjoy its nutty flavor as much as the color it brings to the plate. I use an organic red rice from the Camargue, a region in the southeast of France that's wedged between the two arms of the Rhône river as it flows into the Mediterranean, an exceptionally rich and beautiful marshland, popular with flamingos, mosquitoes, and horses that roam around semi-freely.

1. Set up a steamer. Steam the green beans, tightly covered, until just cooked through but not limp, 7 to 8 minutes. Set aside to cool. The beans can be cooked the day before.

2. In a large salad bowl, whisk together the almond butter, olive oil, lemon juice, vinegar, and salt.

3. Add the cooked beans and turn them gently in the dressing to coat. Stir in the rice. Taste and adjust the seasoning. The salad may be made a few hours in advance up to this point. Cover and refrigerate.

RECIPE CONTINUES

4. Just before serving, add the chopped almonds and parsley, sprinkle with black pepper, and toss to combine.

HARICOTS VERTS

Look for slender haricots verts that feel firm to the touch and have no dark or discolored spots. The wispy little tail can be left on; only the stem end needs trimming and it should break off with a snap. Once trimmed, rinsed, and thoroughly dried, green beans can be packed in an airtight bag and placed in the freezer for later use. They can then be boiled or steamed directly, without thawing.

TOASTING NUTS AND SEEDS

The flavor of nuts and seeds is significantly bolstered when they're toasted. Preheat your oven to 350°F. / 175°C. Spread the nuts (shelled, but whole) or seeds on a baking sheet in a single layer. Roast in the oven, keeping a close eye on them, until golden and fragrant, about 10 minutes. Exact timing depends on the size and moisture content of the nuts or seeds. Alternatively, nuts and seeds can be toasted in a dry skillet over medium heat, shaking the pan regularly; this is more convenient for a small amount, but the result is less even than oven toasting.

EGGPLANT AND FRESH HERB TABBOULEH

Taboulé d'aubergine aux herbes fraîches

I have a great fondness for the North African style of making tabbouleh, which calls for couscous rather than the Middle Eastern bulgur wheat, and uses a greater proportion of grain to herb for a more filling salad. The classic *taboulé* revolves around tomatoes, cucumbers, and mint, but I prefer this eggplant version, spiked with a mix of herbs and a sesame dressing.

Throughout the summer I'll make salads like this one to serve as my workday lunches, taking advantage of how effortless it is to prepare couscous: I'll make a big bowl early in the week, and eat my way through it on subsequent days. But this particular tabbouleh is fit for a crowd, too; I always serve it at the party I throw for my birthday every July.

1. Cut the eggplants into ⅓-inch / 8 mm dice. Put in a colander, sprinkle with 1 teaspoon salt, toss to coat, and let rest for 1 hour. This will help remove any bitterness. Turn out onto a clean kitchen towel and squeeze gently to absorb the juices.

2. Set up a steamer. Steam the eggplant, tightly covered, until very tender but still holding their shape, about 12 minutes. Set aside to cool. This can be done a day ahead and the eggplants refrigerated.

3. In a large heatproof salad bowl, combine the couscous and onion. Stir in the olive oil and 1 teaspoon salt. Pour the boiling water over the couscous. Cover and let stand until the water is absorbed, about 10 minutes

SERVES 8

1½ pounds / 680 g small eggplants

Fine sea salt

2 cups (12 ounces / 340 g) whole wheat couscous

1 small red onion (4¼ ounces / 120 g), finely diced

2 tablespoons extra-virgin olive oil

2 cups / 480 ml boiling water

1 rounded tablespoon all-natural tahini

1 tablespoon harissa, homemade (page 212) or store-bought, or more to taste

¼ cup / 60 ml freshly squeezed lemon juice

1 cup / 30 g sliced fresh mint leaves

1 cup / 30 g sliced fresh basil leaves

1 cup / 30 g chopped fresh cilantro leaves

summer • l'été **69**

(or according to package directions). Fluff with a fork and set aside to cool.

4. In a small bowl, combine the tahini, harissa, and ½ teaspoon salt. Stir in the lemon juice, 1 teaspoon at a time, making sure it is incorporated before adding the next to prevent curdling. Add 2 tablespoons water and stir until smooth. You want a dressing that's pourable, but not too thin; add a little more water as necessary. Taste and adjust the seasoning.

5. Pour the dressing over the couscous and toss to combine. Fold in the eggplant and mint, basil, and cilantro. Taste and adjust the seasoning. Cover and refrigerate until ready to serve. The salad will keep for a few days.

pantry gem

TAHINI

Tahini is made by grinding hulled sesame seeds until they release their oils and turn into an off-white, creamy paste with a nutty flavor and a delicate hint of bitterness. It is used extensively all around the Mediterranean and is the perfect ingredient for thickening sauces and dressings or jazzing up dips and soups. It goes well with apple slices for a snack, too.

You'll find it in natural foods stores and Middle Eastern markets. All tahinis are not created equal, so it may be worth trying different brands until you find the one you prefer; it should be nutty and delicately sweet, with no harsh bitter notes. Get one that's all-natural, containing just sesame seeds, and don't be tempted by "whole" sesame butter made from unhulled seeds; it is more nutritious, but significantly more bitter, too.

Olive oil for cooking

**1 small yellow onion
(4¼ ounces / 120 g),
finely sliced**

**2 garlic cloves,
1 minced, 1 halved**

**10 fresh sage leaves,
midveins removed,
finely sliced**

Fine sea salt

**2½ pounds / 1 kg
tomatoes, roughly
chopped**

**10 ounces / 280 g
stale country or
sourdough bread**

**4 cups / 1 liter
Vegetable Stock
(page 198)**

Hot sauce

**Freshly ground
black pepper**

**¼ cup / 10 g fresh
tarragon or basil
leaves**

TOMATO AND TARRAGON BREAD SOUP

Panade de tomate à l'estragon

We consume a fair amount of bread in my house, and yet I feel I am invariably left with staling end slices no one will eat. It would be unthinkable to throw them out, so I freeze them instead until I have enough to make bread pudding in the winter or this chunky tomato soup in the summer.

Panade is the French word for any peasant-style stew or soup made substantial by the addition of bread (*pain* and *panade* share the same root). This one is a rustic preparation of chopped tomatoes cooked in broth with onions and sage. I serve it for dinner in the summer; if there is a slight chill in the night air, it's especially restorative.

This recipe can only sing as beautifully as the tomatoes you put in it, so use the tastiest field tomatoes possible, in season and ripe, preferably from the farmers' market. Bonus points if you can mix and match different varieties. I garnish this soup with fresh tarragon, an herb with long, thin leaves whose subtly aniseed-like notes lift the overall flavor by a few notches.

1. Heat 1 tablespoon oil in a soup pot over medium heat and add the onion, minced garlic, sage, and a pinch of salt. Cook, stirring often to avoid coloring, until the onion has softened, about 3 minutes. Add the tomatoes, with their juices and seeds, and 1 teaspoon salt.

2. Cut one-third of the bread into slices about ⅓ inch / 8 mm thick and set aside; you'll be making croutons

with those in a moment. Cut the remaining bread into rough cubes and add them to the pot.

3. Pour in the stock, bring to a simmer, cover, and cook until the tomatoes and bread are very soft, about 30 minutes.

4. Add a few dashes of hot sauce, then taste and adjust the seasoning.

5. Toast the reserved slices of bread and, while still warm, rub both sides with the cut side of the halved garlic clove. Dice into croutons.

6. Ladle the soup into bowls. Sprinkle with black pepper, top with croutons, and sprinkle with tarragon. Serve immediately.

SERVES 4

1⅓ cups / 140 g chickpea flour (see opposite)

1 teaspoon fine sea salt

1 teaspoon ground cumin

Olive oil for cooking

Freshly ground black pepper

CHICKPEA GALETTE
Socca

A staple of Nice's culinary heritage, *socca* is a thin crêpe made with chickpea flour and baked on giant copper pans in wood-fired ovens. The large round is sliced into smaller pieces that receive a drizzle of olive oil and a shower of black pepper before they're eaten, hot, with one's fingers. It would be sacrilegious to use cutlery.

Though the wood-fire smokiness does a lot to contribute to socca's addictive flavor, those of us who don't have such an oven can nonetheless make it—or one of its relations—at home. Socca has various siblings around the Mediterranean, such as the Italian *cecina* and *farinata,* or the cumin-flavored *calentita* that Spanish Jews brought with them to North Africa. And although cumin is untraditional in socca, I tried adding some to a batch recently and have never looked back.

Aside from baking socca to serve with a predinner drink, I also make a slightly thicker version to use as a tart base, topped with summertime vegetables, as for the Zucchini and Apricot Socca Tart on page 76.

1. In a medium bowl, combine the chickpea flour, salt, cumin, and 3 tablespoons oil. Pour in 1 cup / 240 ml cold water in a slow stream, whisking constantly to avoid lumps. The mixture will be thinner than pancake batter. Cover and let rest for 2 hours at room temperature, or overnight in the fridge.

2. Place a well-seasoned 10-inch / 25 cm cast-iron pan in the oven and preheat the oven to 400°F. / 200°C.

3. Whisk the batter again. Remove the pan from the oven cautiously (it will be hot) and pour in a good glug of oil, swirling the pan around to coat. Add half

of the batter to the pan and swirl to cover the entire surface. Return to the oven and bake until set, 10 to 15 minutes. Switch the oven to the broiler setting and leave the pan in, keeping a close eye on it, until golden brown and crisp at the top, a few minutes more.

4. Turn the socca out onto a plate—you may have to help it out with a thin spatula—and then flip it back onto a cutting board, browned side up. Cut into square servings with a knife or pizza wheel, drizzle with a little more olive oil, sprinkle with black pepper, and serve hot.

5. Repeat with the remaining batter.

TO USE AS A TART BASE
Prepare the batter as instructed above, but add only ¾ cup / 180 ml water. Pour the entire amount of batter into the pan at once and bake until set, 25 to 30 minutes, before switching to the broiler setting for another 10 minutes.

Turn the socca out onto a plate, then flip it back onto a serving dish, and garnish with cooked or raw vegetables.

Variation Sprinkle thinly sliced scallions (white and green parts) on the batter just after pouring into the hot pan.

pantry gem

CHICKPEA FLOUR

Chickpeas are the poor man's protein all around the Mediterranean rim, and chickpea flour—also called garbanzo flour, gram flour, or *besan*—is the key ingredient for making socca in Nice. In Marseille, it is combined with water and cooked like polenta, then cooled and cut into fingers that are fried and sold as panisses from street carts by the old port. Chickpea flour can be added in small quantities to breads and cakes, and it is a component of some gluten-free flour mixes.

**9 ounces / 250 g
apricots or yellow
peaches, pitted
and diced**

**1 small / 120 g
zucchini**

**Socca tart base
(pages 74–75)**

Flaky sea salt

**Freshly ground
black pepper**

**1 teaspoon fresh
thyme leaves**

ZUCCHINI AND APRICOT SOCCA TART

Tarte socca courgette et abricot

When I am able to find young, tender zucchini, be they green or yellow, I like to cut them into slices with my trusty mandoline and use them raw to garnish savory tarts, scattering the paper-thin rounds over it with as little direction as possible, as if I'd dropped a deck of cards. The effect is fresh and pretty.

I build this zucchini tart on a crust inspired by socca, the delicious chickpea flour galette from Nice. On the tart base I spread a layer of fresh apricot compote, whose acidity bolsters the bright sweetness of the raw zucchini slices. It's an unusual combination but a successful one.

You can serve this in wedges as a first or main course, but it's just as well received cut into nibble-size pieces and paired with a glass of rosé from Provence.

1. Cook the diced apricots in a small saucepan over medium-low heat, uncovered, until very soft, about 10 minutes. Increase the heat, bring to a simmer, and cook for another 5 minutes to thicken slightly. Set aside to cool completely. You should have about 6 tablespoons of the apricot compote.

2. Using a mandoline slicer or very sharp knife, cut the zucchini into paper-thin slices.

3. Place the socca browned side up on a serving dish and spread with the apricot compote. Scatter the zucchini slices on top and sprinkle with salt, pepper, and the thyme.

4. Cut with a serrated knife and serve.

Olive Oil Tart Dough (page 200)

1 large organic egg, separated

1¾ pounds / 800 g plum tomatoes

Fine sea salt

1 tablespoon olive oil for cooking

2 small red onions (4¼ ounces / 120 g each), thinly sliced

2 tablespoons strong Dijon mustard

Handful of fresh basil leaves, purple if available, torn

Freshly ground black pepper

TOMATO MUSTARD TART
Tarte tomate et moutarde

In my late teens, none of my friends knew much about cooking, but we each had a simple dish or two that we could be trusted to make, mostly savory tarts we baked with prerolled puff pastry from the supermarket. One day, for a birthday dinner, a friend decided to serve a tomato tart. We bought canned tomatoes and a jar of mustard to spread over the crust, as the classic French recipe goes.

It was a fine-looking tart, but at the first bite we started to tear up, fiery fumes burning up our sinuses. French mustard can be quite strong, especially when the jar is freshly opened, and the budding cook had been a little overenthusiastic spreading it on. Not wanting to upset our friend, we pretended it was quite all right and sniffled our way through it bravely, but I always think of her when I prepare a tomato tart; I make sure I go easy on the mustard, using it to enhance the tomatoes—not to induce tears.

My grown-up version calls for fresh tomatoes rather than canned and instead of store-bought pastry, I use my trusted Olive Oil Tart Dough, which does a better job of withstanding the juices seeping from the tomatoes.

1. Preheat the oven to 325°F. / 160°C.

2. Prepare and blind-bake the crust in an 11- to 12-inch / 28 to 30 cm tart pan, brushing it with some of the egg white (see page 200).

3. Halve the tomatoes, carve out the core, and remove the juice and seeds. (Save them for drinking later, with a bit of salt and olive oil.) Sprinkle the cut sides with salt and place the tomatoes cut-side down in a colander, so more juices will drain out.

4. Heat the oil in a medium saucepan over medium-low heat. Add the onions and ½ teaspoon salt and cook, stirring often to prevent coloring, until the onions are very soft, about 15 minutes. Let cool slightly.

5. Stir the egg yolk, any remaining egg white, and the mustard into the onions and spread over the crust. Arrange the halved tomatoes, cut-side down, over the onion layer. Bake until the tomatoes are cooked through and wrinkled, about 45 minutes.

6. Top with the basil and black pepper. Cut slices with a serrated knife and serve.

1 cup / 200 g pearl
barley

2 cups / 300 g
shucked fresh shell
beans (from about
1 pound / 450 g shell
beans in the pod) or
1 cup / 200 g dried
white or flageolet
beans

Olive oil for cooking

1 small yellow onion
(4¼ ounces / 120 g),
chopped

3 garlic cloves,
minced

Fine sea salt

15 fresh sage
leaves, minced

Extra-virgin olive oil

Freshly ground
black pepper

Aged Parmesan or
other hard cheese,
cut into shavings
with a vegetable
peeler (optional)

FRESH SHELL BEANS AND BARLEY WITH SAGE AND GARLIC

Haricots à écosser et orge à la sauge et à l'ail

Most cooks are familiar with the humble yet glorious bean in its dried form, but few stop to ponder that it was once fresh. Labeled as cranberry beans, cannellini, or lima beans, these shell beans appear in market stalls in mid- to late summer, sheathed in pods that may be white, green, or streaked with pink. It's worth seeking them out: they're quick to shuck and the beans can be cooked without soaking, in much less time than their dried counterparts. They are also sweeter in flavor and their texture is creamy, without ever turning mealy or mushy.

Combined with pearl barley and flavored with fresh sage and garlic, they make a nutritious and satisfying dish that may be served warm or cool, with a little cheese on top if you like. If shell beans are unavailable, or out of season, dried beans can be substituted.

1. Soak the barley overnight in a large bowl with water to cover by about 1 inch / 2.5 cm. (If using dried beans, soak them the same way in a separate bowl.)

2. The next day, drain and rinse the barley and cook according to package directions until tender but still retaining its shape. (Pearl barley usually needs to simmer in salted water for 25 to 45 minutes, or 15 to 25 minutes in a pressure cooker.)

3. In a separate pot, combine the shell beans and 4 cups / 1 liter cold water. Bring to a simmer, cover, and cook, stirring from time to time, until tender, about 20 minutes. (If using dried beans, drain, rinse,

and simmer for 45 minutes to 1½ hours, or 25 to
40 minutes in a pressure cooker.)

4. Heat 1 tablespoon cooking olive oil in a large skillet
   over medium heat. Add the onion, garlic, and a
   sprinkle of salt, and cook, stirring often, until softened
   and fragrant, about 4 minutes.

5. Drain the beans and barley and add to the skillet
   with the sage and 1½ teaspoons salt. Cook for a few
   minutes, allowing the sage to soften and the flavors to
   meld. Taste and adjust the seasoning.

6. Add a drizzle of extra-virgin olive oil, sprinkle with
   black pepper and cheese (if using), and serve warm,
   cold, or use as a filling for the Stuffed Vegetables on
   page 83.

pantry gem

DRIED BEANS

I can't be more emphatic about the benefits of keeping a bag of dried beans in
your pantry. They are cheap, tasty, and nutritious, and despite their reputation,
they don't take much effort to cook from scratch—just a little foresight to soak
them overnight. If you are willing to invest in a pressure cooker, it will shorten the
cooking time significantly; to save even more time, I always make a double batch
and freeze the half I don't need, still in its cooking broth, for later use.

Buy your beans from a source that has a good turnover: although beans have
a virtually eternal shelf life, they get tougher over time and will take much longer
to cook.

STUFFED VEGETABLES WITH BEANS AND BARLEY

Petits farcis aux haricots et à l'orge

Petits farcis niçois are a traditional recipe from Provence: assorted summer vegetables—tomatoes, onions, zucchini, mini pattypans, and the like—are hollowed out, garnished with a meat-based stuffing, and roasted in the oven. I am quite smitten with the concept of stuffed vegetables; they make for a fun preparation process, and a good-looking dish. But I forgo the classic meat stuffing in favor of grains and legumes, which do a wonderful job of both satisfying the appetite and enhancing the flavors of the vegetable shells they fill.

You could dream up an infinity of worthy fillings; here, I use Fresh Shell Beans and Barley with Sage and Garlic.

1. Peel the papery outer layer off the onions. Trim the root end by slicing off a thin layer of flesh, just enough to give the onions a flat base to sit on, but maintaining their round shape. Slice off a "hat" at the stem end, and use a melon baller to carve out the insides so they form little round cups to hold the stuffing. (Use the onion flesh you've carved out in the fresh shell beans recipe on page 80, or save for stock; see page 198.)

2. If you're using round zucchini, prepare them in the same fashion, slicing off a hat at the stem end and carving out the insides. If you're using elongated zucchini, halve them lengthwise and carve to form slender canoes.

RECIPE CONTINUES

6 small red onions (4¼ ounces / 120 g each)

6 small zucchini, round or elongated (4¼ ounces / 120 g each)

6 small round tomatoes (4¼ ounces / 120 g each)

Fine sea salt

Freshly ground black pepper

5 tablespoons pine nuts, toasted (see page 68)

2 large organic eggs, lightly beaten

Fresh Shell Beans and Barley with Sage and Garlic (page 80)

Olive oil for cooking

3. Slice off a hat from the tops of the tomatoes and carve out their insides. (Save the flesh and juices for eating later, with a bit of salt and olive oil.) Sprinkle the insides with salt and set them upside down on a plate for the excess juices to drain out.

4. Bring salted water to a boil in a large pot. Add the hollowed-out onions and simmer until just tender, about 8 minutes. Lift them out with a slotted spoon and set them upside down in a colander to drain. Add the zucchini hats and onion hats to the pot and simmer until just tender, about 3 minutes. Drain thoroughly.

5. Preheat the oven to 425°F. / 220°C.

6. Arrange the vegetables in a single layer, hollowed-side up, in 1 large or 2 medium baking dishes. Sprinkle with pepper.

7. Stir the pine nuts and eggs into the bean and barley mixture and pack into the vegetables. Place a matching hat on each of the vegetables (except for the elongated zucchini) and drizzle with oil.

8. Bake, basting the vegetables with their own juices (and switching the position of the baking dishes halfway through if you're using two), until tender and lightly browned, about 40 minutes.

9. Serve hot or just slightly warm.

CORSICAN BELL PEPPER STEW
Pebronata

MAKES ABOUT
2 CUPS / 480 ML

Pebronata is a Corsican stew of bell peppers and tomatoes that is traditionally intended as a sauce for roasted meats but is flavorsome enough to stand on its own two feet. A simple but vibrant preparation, it fares beautifully when served hot over a bowl of rice or pasta, or cold, on a toasted slice of good sourdough bread, with a poached egg and a bit of shaved hard cheese on top. You can also use it as a filling for savory Pebronata Canelés (page 90).

Pebronata improves as it sits, so make it a day ahead if you can. If you have leftover red wine from the night before, the stew benefits from a good splash, but I wouldn't open a bottle just for that purpose.

1 tablespoon **olive oil** for cooking

2 small **red onions** (4¼ ounces / 120 g each), finely sliced

1 **garlic clove**, minced

Fine sea salt

3 medium / 540 g red **bell peppers**, diced

1 teaspoon chopped **rosemary**, preferably fresh

3 **juniper berries**, crushed with the side of a chef's knife

2 **plum tomatoes**, diced

¼ cup / 60 ml **red wine** (optional)

Freshly ground black pepper

1. Heat the oil in a medium saucepan over medium heat. Add the onions, garlic, and a pinch of salt, and cook, stirring often to avoid coloring, until softened, 4 minutes.

2. Add the bell peppers, rosemary, and juniper berries. Season with salt, stir, and reduce the heat to medium-low. Cook, uncovered, stirring often, until very soft, 20 to 30 minutes.

3. Add the tomatoes along with their seeds and juices and the red wine (if using). Add a little more salt and cook until the tomatoes have melted into the sauce and the juices have reduced, another 10 to 20 minutes.

4. Season generously with black pepper, then taste and adjust the seasoning.

SERVES 6

Fine sea salt

1⅓ pounds / 600 g small eggplants

3 teaspoons herbes de Provence or a mix of dried thyme, rosemary, basil, and/or oregano

1⅓ pounds / 600 g medium zucchini

1¾ pounds / 800 g plum tomatoes

Olive oil for cooking

2 small yellow onions (4¼ ounces / 120 g each), finely sliced

8 fresh sage leaves, minced

2 garlic cloves, minced

RATATOUILLE TIAN
Tian ratatouille

Every French cook I know who went to see the animated film *Ratatouille* came out of the cinema saying, "Fun movie, but that ratatouille was really a *tian*," referring to the sequence when the eponymous dish is served to Anton Ego, the restaurant critic.

The two dishes do have things in common: their region of origin (Provence) and some of the market-fresh produce they call for (tomatoes, zucchini, onions, eggplants). But while the vegetables are cooked in chunks and on the stovetop for a classic ratatouille, it is the tian that introduces those pretty overlapping rows of thinly sliced vegetables and the oven roasting that coaxes them into caramelization.

Named after the earthenware pan it is traditionally baked in, a tian is a gorgeous dish that melds the flavors of the vegetables into a warmly sweet ensemble, perfect for serving with a side of Blanch-Roasted New Potatoes (page 23). It tastes even better the next day, reheated or cold, over a bowl of long-grain rice or slipped inside a focaccia sandwich with fresh basil and pine nuts. Note that this dish looks best if the vegetable slices are all approximately the same diameter; so keep that in mind when you're choosing them at the greenmarket.

1. An hour before you plan to cook, salt the eggplants to remove any trace of bitterness: using a mandoline slicer or very sharp knife, cut the eggplants crosswise into ⅛-inch / 3 mm rounds. Put them in a colander, sprinkle with 1 teaspoon salt, and toss to coat. Let rest for 1 hour to allow some of the moisture to be drawn out of the slices. Pat dry with a clean kitchen towel. Transfer to a bowl and sprinkle with 1 teaspoon of the herbes de Provence.

RECIPE CONTINUES

2. Cut the zucchini and tomatoes crosswise into ⅛-inch / 3 mm rounds. Place in two separate bowls and sprinkle each with ½ teaspoon salt and 1 teaspoon of the herbes de Provence.

3. Preheat the oven to 350° F. / 175° C.

4. Lightly oil an 8 × 10-inch / 20 × 25 cm glass or ceramic baking dish. Scatter the sliced onions evenly over the bottom. Sprinkle with ¼ teaspoon salt and a touch of olive oil.

5. Arrange a row of overlapping zucchini slices along one side of the dish. Pack them in tightly so that they are almost upright. Sprinkle with a little sage and garlic. Follow with a row of overlapping tomato slices and then a row of eggplant slices, sprinkling each with a little sage and garlic as you go. Repeat the pattern until you've filled the dish and used up all the vegetables, packing the rows of vegetables together very tightly. If you have vegetables remaining at the end, slip them among their peers to flesh out the rows that seem to need it.

6. Drizzle with 3 tablespoons olive oil, cover loosely with foil, and bake for 30 minutes.

7. Increase the oven temperature to 425°F. / 220°C. and bake for another 30 minutes.

8. Remove the foil and bake until the vegetables are tender and the tips of the vegetable slices are appealingly browned, about another 30 minutes. Serve hot, at room temperature, or chilled.

PRESERVED LEMONS
Citrons confits

MAKES ONE
1-PINT / 480 ML
JAR

**3 small / 270 g
organic lemons**

**⅓ cup / 85 g
coarse salt**

**1 tablespoon
coriander seeds**

**1 cup / 240 ml
lemon juice (freshly
squeezed or bottled)**

Preserving lemons in salt and their own juices for a few weeks makes their rind soften and their flavor deepen. The acidity becomes much tamer and you're left with a complex pickle, both lemony and sour, that is a popular ingredient in Moroccan cuisine and a fantastic condiment. With it you'll jazz up vegetable stews and soups; rice, lentil, and couscous dishes; dips, spreads, marinades, and salads, such as Shaved Fennel Salad (page 65). You'll be using the rind, so buy organic lemons.

1. Have ready a clean 1-pint / 480 ml glass jar with a tight-fitting lid. Rinse the jar and lid with boiling water and then put upside down on a clean kitchen towel to dry.

2. Wash the lemons well and cut lengthwise into quarters. Toss in a medium bowl with half of the salt.

3. Put a little of the remaining salt at the bottom of the jar and start filling the jar with the lemon quarters, packing them tightly, and adding coriander seeds and more of the salt between each layer.

4. When the jar is full, pour in lemon juice to cover the lemons entirely. Close the jar tightly and put it away somewhere cool and dark for 3 weeks, shaking the jar every few days. The rinds will gradually become more translucent and the juice syrupy. Once open, transfer the jar to the fridge and use within a few weeks.

5. To use, gently pull the pulp and pith off the rind and discard them. Dice or slice the rind and add to the dish as it cooks or as a finishing touch.

3 large organic eggs

**¾ cup / 100 g
all-purpose flour**

**1 teaspoon fine
sea salt**

**½ cup / 120 ml
milk (not skim)
or unflavored,
unsweetened
nondairy milk**

**Corsican Bell
Pepper Stew
(page 85), cooled**

PEBRONATA CANELÉS
Canelés à la pebronata

The original *canelé* is a small sweet cake from Bordeaux; the rum
and vanilla batter is baked in its characteristic high molds with
ridges all around until the outside becomes darkly caramelized
and crisp while the inside remains chewy and custardy.

The signature shape lends itself to savory preparations, too,
and I use my canelé molds to bake three-bite, golden nibbles
whose texture can be likened to that of a crustless quiche. They
are ideal for picnics, brunches, and buffet spreads; they taste
good warm or at room temperature, and are easy to eat with
one's fingers without making a mess on one's floral print dress.
I've developed a go-to formula for the basic batter, into which
I fold whatever ingredients strike my fancy: raw or cooked
vegetables, cheeses, herbs, and spices. In this version, the canelés
are flavored with *pebronata*, the Corsican bell pepper stew.

1. Preheat the oven to 400°F. / 200°C. and have ready
   a tray of silicone canelé molds. (Bouchon molds,
   a mini-muffin tin, or a regular muffin tin may be
   substituted; grease them very well if they aren't
   nonstick or silicone.)

2. In a medium bowl with a pouring spout, beat the eggs
   with a fork. Beat in the flour and salt. Pour in the milk
   and beat until combined. Fold in the bell pepper stew.

3. Pour into the molds, stopping about ⅓ inch / 8 mm
   from the top. Bake until golden, 35 to 45 minutes.
   (If you're using something other than canelé molds,
   you may have to increase or decrease the baking time
   depending on their size.) As they bake, the canelés will

puff up and then settle down. If the tops seem to be browning too quickly, cover loosely with foil. Let cool in the molds for 5 to 10 minutes before turning out.

4. Serve warm or at room temperature. The canelés can be frozen after cooling: place them on a tray in the freezer and collect in a freezer bag when completely frozen. To reheat, arrange the frozen canelés on a baking sheet and place in a 350°F. / 175°C. oven for 15 minutes, or until warm.

PEACH, ALMOND, AND CARDAMOM CLAFOUTIS
Clafoutis de pêches, amande et cardamome

Throughout the months of July and August, a large portion of my energy is devoted to keeping us in peaches and nectarines: finding the tastiest ones, grown in the South of France; identifying the most colorful and fragrant specimens from each crate; carrying them home as carefully as I would a newborn; and eating them in order of ripening, watching out for any sign of spoilage and waging a merciless war against fruit flies.

Despite my not insignificant efforts, every once in a while I get a bad batch—the mealy kind that make your teeth protest and are neither sweet nor aromatic enough to satisfy. Fortunately, I have a redemption recipe for those: a clafoutis that turns them into a delicious dessert, bolstering their flavor with almonds and cardamom, and cradling them in a delicately sweet batter that camouflages their texture.

No need to mention you've cleverly used up your less-than-perfect peaches; no one will ever know. And, of course, if all you have is good peaches, they will perform splendidly in this recipe, too.

SERVES 8

4 green cardamom pods or ½ teaspoon ground green cardamom

⅔ cup / 85 g almond flour

½ cup / 65 g all-purpose flour

½ cup / 100 g unrefined blond cane sugar (also sold as evaporated cane juice)

1 tablespoon cornstarch

3 large organic eggs

¾ cup / 180 ml unflavored, unsweetened almond milk or dairy milk (not skim)

2¼ pounds / 1 kg peaches, yellow, white, or a mix

Crème fraîche or all-natural Greek yogurt (optional)

1. Pop the cardamom pods open with the flat of a chef's knife and grind the seeds finely with a mortar and pestle.

2. In a medium bowl, combine the almond flour, all-purpose flour, sugar, cornstarch, and ground cardamom. Break the eggs into the bowl and whisk until combined. Pour in the milk in a thin stream, whisking all the while to incorporate.

RECIPE CONTINUES

3. Preheat the oven to 350°F. / 175° C.

4. Pit the peaches, cut them into slices without peeling, and arrange on the bottom of a greased 8-inch/20 cm square glass or ceramic baking dish. (Alternatively, use individual baking dishes.)

5. Pour the batter evenly over the peaches. Bake until set and golden, 30 to 40 minutes (20 to 30 minutes for individual dishes).

6. Serve slightly warm, at room temperature, or cold, with an optional dollop of crème fraîche or Greek yogurt. The leftovers do well at breakfast.

pantry gem

STAR ANISE AND GREEN CARDAMOM

Whole star anise and green cardamom pods can be purchased from ethnic markets, gourmet stores, or online spice stores. They keep for years, unlike their ground counterparts, and find their place in many dishes, sweet and savory. Star anise pairs well with carrots, zucchini, melon, figs, pears, and oranges; green cardamom with winter squash, eggplant, egg dishes, chickpeas, lentils and rice, chocolate, citrus, stone fruits, and persimmons.

SOUR CHERRY AND ROSE COMPOTE

Compote de griottes à la rose

MAKES 1½ CUPS / 360 ML

1 pound / 450 g pitted sour cherries

½ cup / 100 g unrefined blond cane sugar (also sold as evaporated cane juice)

1 to 2 tablespoons rosewater or orange flower water (optional), to taste

In a short story titled "Les Vieux" (the old folks) drawn from Daudet's *Letters from My Windmill,* the narrator visits a friend's grandparents in the countryside as a favor to the friend who lives far away and can't see them regularly.

He is greeted with the same warmth as if he himself were the prodigal grandchild and they fuss over him as only grandparents will. They insist on opening a jar of sour cherries in eau-de-vie that the grandmother put up some time ago and had set aside for her grandson who loves them so.

Only she is old and forgetful and it soon becomes apparent that she has not added any sugar at all. The cherries are atrocious, but the narrator eats his entire cup without a peep.

This tale of filial love by proxy moves me to tears and I cannot buy sour cherries without thinking of Mamette, the grandmother in the story. I've never been fond of sour cherries in eau-de-vie myself, but I do love to make compotes out of them. I add a touch of rosewater and find the mix of sweet, sour, and floral flavors delightful. Serve over yogurt, ice cream, or Savoy Sponge Cake (page 97).

1. In a medium saucepan, combine the cherries, sugar, and ¼ cup / 60 ml water. Bring to a simmer over medium heat and cook, stirring often, for 5 minutes.

2. Lift the cherries out of the pan and into a bowl with a slotted spoon. Turn the heat to high, bring the juices to a boil, and cook until syrupy, 3 to 5 minutes.

3. Pour the syrup over the cherries and stir in 1 tablespoon rosewater, or more to taste. Serve warm or chilled.

SAVOY SPONGE CAKE
Biscuit de Savoie

I once had the opportunity to lunch at a very old restaurant of great renown in Paris. My companion and I were excited, our imaginations racing with dreams of delicate dishes, plush chairs, and graceful service. We were to have none of that, except for the chairs, which gave us no complaint. We were rushed through a meal that sorely lacked sparkle, glasses of wine were brought to us out of order, and an insensitive comment was made about my friend's coat.

The one redeeming component of this lunch debacle was the slice of *biscuit de Savoie* that was produced at the end of the meal: a thin wedge of pale-crumbed sponge cake on a plain white plate. The bites that we tore from it landed on our tongues with a soothing sigh.

Biscuit de Savoie is thought to have been invented in the kitchens of the Count of Savoy in the middle of the fourteenth century and has been delighting gourmets ever since with its light, mousse-like texture and subtle citrus notes. It is a fine breakfast or tea cake, but I like to serve it for dessert as well, with a fruity dancing partner, such as Sour Cherry and Rose Compote (page 95).

SERVES 8

6 large organic eggs, separated

1¼ cups / 250 g unrefined blond cane sugar (also sold as evaporated cane juice), plus more for sprinkling

Grated zest of 1 organic lemon

1 tablespoon orange flower water

1¼ cups / 150 g cake flour

⅓ cup / 55 g potato starch or cornstarch

A pat of unsalted butter, for the pan

¼ teaspoon fine sea salt

⅛ teaspoon cream of tartar

Confectioners' sugar, for dusting (optional)

1. In the bowl of a stand mixer fitted with the whisk attachment, or by hand with a whisk, beat the egg yolks with the sugar and lemon zest until smooth and pale yellow. Add the orange flower water. Sift together the flour and starch and fold into the egg mixture with a spatula; the batter will be stiff.

2. Preheat the oven to 350°F. / 175°C. Grease a 10-inch / 25 cm fluted tube pan (the kind you would use for a Bundt cake) with butter and sprinkle the inside

RECIPE CONTINUES

with sugar. This buttering and sugaring should be done regardless of the type of pan you use—nonstick or not—but if it isn't nonstick, grease the pan *very* thoroughly so the cake will unmold without drama.

3. In the bowl of a stand mixer fitted with the whisk attachment, beat the egg whites with the salt and cream of tartar until they form stiff peaks. Stir one-fourth of the egg whites into the batter, stirring them in with a spatula to loosen the batter. Fold in another fourth of the egg whites, working more gently now and lifting the preparation with the spatula to avoid deflating the egg whites. Repeat with the remaining egg whites in two additions.

4. Pour into the prepared pan and sprinkle the surface with a little more sugar. Bake until the top is golden and springy to the touch and a knife inserted into the cake comes out clean, 25 to 30 minutes. Avoid overbaking.

5. Run a knife around the cake to loosen, then turn out onto a rack, and let cool completely. Dust with confectioners' sugar, if desired.

— *pantry gem* —

ORANGE FLOWER WATER

Orange flower water, also called orange blossom water, is a clear liquid distilled from the flowers of bitter orange trees. This wonderfully fresh and aromatic ingredient is popular in the Middle East and all around the Mediterranean, including France. You'll find it in Middle Eastern markets and gourmet grocery stores. Used with a light hand, it brings subtle floral notes to desserts (such as compotes or the Fruit Salad with Spiced Syrup on page 190), baked goods (such as madeleines or focaccia), and drinks (such as fruit juices or cocktails). In Lebanon, it is added to piping hot sweetened water to make "white coffee," and it can be used as a perfume; just dab a little of it behind your ears.

YOGURT MOUSSE WITH RASPBERRIES

Fontainebleau aux framboises

My first brush with *fontainebleau* was at an old, beautifully preserved cheese shop in my neighborhood, where I noticed pretty bundles of cheesecloth filled with an off-white mousse. The cheese lady explained that fontainebleau was a classic preparation named after the city outside of Paris and a specialty of theirs: a mousse made of fromage blanc (a French yogurt-like dairy product) and whipped cream that you eat with a sprinkle of sugar and a few berries.

I bought a couple and we feasted on them that night, discovering what it would feel like to eat a cloud made of milk. I soon attempted to make my own and found it easy. With a handful of fresh raspberries and possibly a drizzle of Lemon Verbena Syrup, it makes for a quietly elegant dessert.

Fromage blanc is hard to find outside of France, but plain yogurt may be used instead. If you have access to artisanal dairy products, this is the perfect opportunity to let those excellent yogurts and creams shine.

1. Line a medium fine-mesh sieve with a 4-layer piece of cheesecloth and set over a deep bowl.

2. In a medium bowl, combine the yogurt and salt.

3. Split the vanilla bean lengthwise with a sharp knife, scrape the seeds from the inside of the bean with the dull side of the blade, and add them to the bowl of a stand mixer fitted with the whisk attachment. Add the

RECIPE CONTINUES

SERVES 6

1 cup / 240 ml plain all-natural **yogurt**

Pinch of **fine sea salt**

½ small fresh **vanilla bean** or 1 teaspoon pure **vanilla extract**

1 cup / 240 ml **heavy cream**

¼ cup / 50 g unrefined blond cane **sugar** (also sold as evaporated cane juice)

1 container (6 ounces / 170 g) fresh **raspberries**, for serving

Lemon Verbena Syrup (page 101), for serving (optional)

cream and whip, starting at low speed and beating faster as it gains volume. When the cream is thick enough that the wire loops of the whisk leave traces, sprinkle in the sugar, beating all the while, until the cream forms peaks.

4. Fold it into the yogurt with a spatula, working in a circular, up-and-down motion to avoid deflating the cream.

5. Pour into the prepared sieve, cover with a plate, and place in the refrigerator to drain for 6 hours or overnight. (Alternatively, scoop the cream mixture into individual pieces of cheesecloth, bundle them up, tie with a string, and leave to drain in the colander.)

6. Scoop the fontainebleau into bowls (or serve in the individual cheesecloth bundles for guests to unwrap) and top with raspberries and lemon verbena syrup (if using). Eat leftovers within a day or two.

LEMON VERBENA SYRUP
Sirop de verveine citronnelle

Lemon verbena is an unusual herb that produces spearhead-shaped leaves with a sweet, intoxicating scent of lime and lemongrass. They make a sensational sorbet and you can add them to fruit salads and jams, or muddle them into your summer cocktails. Look for it at farmers' markets or grow your own. Grind the fresh leaves with sugar to make a lemon verbena sugar that will keep for a long time, or let the leaves dry naturally and put away to make herbal tea in the winter, or steep them into this flavored syrup.

I use this to sweeten the fontainebleau on page 99, or pour it over yogurt, crêpes, pound cakes, or toasted slices of brioche. The same technique may be applied to any other herb you have on hand.

1. In a small saucepan, combine the sugar with 1 cup / 240 ml cold water. Bring to a boil, stirring until the sugar is dissolved, and remove from the heat. Add the lemon verbena, cover, and steep for 1 hour.

2. Filter through a sieve and pour into a clean jar. Refrigerate until ready to use. It will keep for at least 1 month.

MAKES 1¹/₃ CUPS / 320 ML

¾ cup / 150 g sugar

25 fresh lemon verbena leaves, chopped, or dried leaves

SERVES 4

1 ripe and fragrant Charentais melon or cantaloupe (about 2 pounds / 900 g)

1 small knob of fresh ginger, peeled and sliced

1 teaspoon honey, or more to taste

Freshly ground black pepper

8 tiny fresh mint leaves, taken from the tops of the sprigs

MELON AND GINGER SOUP
Soupe de melon au gingembre

Choosing a melon is something of an art form. At good produce stalls in France, the sales attendant will ask when you plan on eating the melon (today, tomorrow, lunch or dinner?) and—after a bit of theatrical appraising, brows furrowed in concentration— will then select the perfect specimen.

Left to my own devices, I rely mostly on my sense of smell, sniffing out the bottom button opposite the stem end: the riper the melon, the fruitier it will smell in that spot. I look for a delicate odor, almost floral. If it smells green, the melon is under- ripe, but if it's just a hint, it can probably be left to ripen on the counter. If, on the other hand, the smell is so strong it's cloying, the melon is past its prime; skip it.

Most of the time, we just split a melon in two and eat it plain, with a spoon, but I find it extra refreshing in the form of a cold soup, spiked with fresh ginger and black pepper. This soup is lovely on its own, with Breton Shortbread Cookies (page 45), or topped with a scoop of vanilla ice cream or Gazelle Horn Sorbet (page 55).

1. Halve the melon and scoop out the seeds and pulp. If the pulp is fleshy and juicy, transfer to a fine-mesh sieve set over a bowl and press it with the back of a spoon to extract as much juice as possible. Discard the seeds.

2. Using a small melon baller, scoop 16 balls of melon flesh and set aside.

3. Scoop out the rest of the flesh with a regular spoon and transfer it with the collected juices to a blender. Add the ginger and honey and whizz until smooth. Taste and add a little more honey as needed. You should get about 2 cups / 480 ml of melon soup.

4. This can be prepared up to 2 hours ahead. Cover the melon balls and melon soup and refrigerate. Give the soup a stir before serving.

5. Divide the melon balls among 4 cups or ramekins (each about ½ cup / 120 ml) and pour in the melon soup. Sprinkle with black pepper, garnish with the mint leaves, and serve.

FALL

L'automne

Fall is the epitome of the transitional season in Paris, as we ease back into the day-to-day rhythm of the city and try not to be saddened by the slow disappearance of sun-ripened produce. Instead, I cheer myself up with the changing colors in market stalls, inviting them into soul-warming dishes, and I seize opportunities to go foraging for the late-season berries and wild mushrooms that can be found in forests just outside of Paris.

The back-to-school vibe spurs new resolves that extend to the kitchen; it's a good time to clear out a cluttered pantry and rethink the way we plan meals. This section presents vegetable dishes to work into your weeknight rotation or to make ahead for relaxed dinner parties.

PRODUCE TO PLAY WITH IN THE FALL

- Apples
- Beets
- Blackberries
- Broccoli
- Brussels sprouts
- Cabbage
- Carrots
- Cauliflower
- Celery root
- Chestnuts
- Endives
- Fennel
- Figs
- Grapefruit
- Grapes
- Kiwifruit
- Kohlrabi
- Leeks
- Lemons
- Mâche
- Mushrooms
- Oranges
- Parsnips
- Pears
- Persimmons
- Plums
- Potatoes
- Quince
- Spinach
- Swiss chard
- Turnips
- Walnuts
- Winter squash

¾ cup / 180 ml
dehydrated mixed
seaweed flakes

1 garlic clove,
finely chopped

2 tablespoons
finely diced shallot

2 tablespoons
freshly squeezed
lemon juice

2 rounded teaspoons
drained capers

3 tablespoons
extra-virgin olive oil

1 tablespoon walnut
oil or untoasted
sesame oil

¼ teaspoon fine
sea salt

Freshly ground
black pepper

SEAWEED TARTARE
Tartare d'algues

Although we haven't reached Japanese heights yet, seaweed consumption is increasingly common in France, and that's not so surprising; the French love flavors from the sea, oysters being considered a supreme delicacy, and with such a wide coastline, the country offers plenty of opportunities to grow and harvest seaweed.

One of the best-loved ways to prepare and eat seaweed is as a *tartare*, a finely chopped and well-seasoned mix of various types of seaweeds. Highly flavorful, and not so strong as to turn off novice seaweed eaters, it can be spread on crackers, thin rounds of baguette, or steamed potato slices to serve with a predinner drink. It can be used as a sandwich spread, too, and to stuff plum tomatoes, top an omelet, or dress a warm potato salad. Prepare the tartare a few hours in advance of serving.

1. Put the seaweed in a bowl with 1 cup / 240 ml cold water. Set aside to rehydrate for 30 minutes.

---

pantry gem

DEHYDRATED SEAWEED FLAKES

If you're focusing on plant foods, seaweed is a great ingredient to mix things up and introduce an unusual complexity of flavor—and nutrition—to your dishes.

Although seaweed can be purchased fresh, dried seaweed is the easiest form to have in your pantry: it keeps well and doesn't need to be de-salted. Look for dehydrated seaweed flakes at natural foods stores, Asian markets, or online and choose a mix of various varieties (such as nori, dulse, wakame, sea lettuce . . .), if available. They are nice sprinkled over a cucumber salad or a bowl of rice or folded into cracker or savory cookie dough.

2. Meanwhile, combine the garlic, shallot, and lemon juice in another bowl; the acidity will soften the raw edge of the garlic and shallot.

3. Drain the seaweed thoroughly, transfer to a food processor, and add the garlic mixture, the capers, both oils, the salt, and a grinding of black pepper. Pulse until finely chopped, scraping down the sides of the bowl regularly. Taste and adjust the seasoning.

4. Transfer to a jar, close tightly, and refrigerate for at least 2 hours or overnight, to allow the flavors to mingle. Eat within 2 to 3 days.

LEEKS VINAIGRETTE
Poireaux vinaigrette

I have a definite fondness for the classic bistro hors d'oeuvre
repertoire: *céleri rémoulade* (grated celery root in mustardy
mayonnaise), *œuf mayonnaise* (deviled egg), *radis beurre* (radishes
with butter), *carottes râpées* (grated carrots in vinaigrette). . . . If
they're made with care and good ingredients, these unassuming
appetizers are considerably more exciting than their names
suggest, and their very simplicity is an opportunity for the
cook's talent to shine.

    Poireaux vinaigrette is an excellent example, a full-flavored,
refreshing note on which to open a meal in the cold season.
Young leeks are sliced into ribbons, steamed, and served with
a drizzle of vinaigrette, a shower of fresh herbs, and some egg
"sprinkles" made by pressing a hard-boiled egg through a
sieve (aka *œuf mimosa,* in reference to the shape and color of
the flower).

1. Cut off the dark tops of the leeks and reserve for stock
   (see Keeping a Stock Box, page 198). Trim and wash
   the leeks (see box on page 165). Cut them lengthwise
   into halves or quarters, depending on their thickness,
   to form long, thin strips. Set up a steamer. Steam the
   leeks, tightly covered, until tender, 10 to 12 minutes.
   Rinse under cold running water and set aside to drain
   and cool. This can be prepared up to a day ahead;
   refrigerate in an airtight container.

2. Follow the instructions on page 206 to make a basic
   vinaigrette with the vinegar, shallot, mustard,
   ¼ teaspoon salt, pepper to taste, and oil. This can be
   prepared ahead; refrigerate in an airtight container.

RECIPE CONTINUES

1½ pounds / 680 g
leeks, the thinner
the better

1 tablespoon red
wine vinegar or
cider vinegar

2 tablespoons
finely diced shallot

1½ teaspoons strong
Dijon mustard

Fine sea salt

Freshly ground
black pepper

3 tablespoons
extra-virgin olive oil

1 hard-boiled large
organic egg, cooled
and peeled

1 cup / 20 g fresh
chervil, flat-leaf
parsley, or cilantro

3. Press the hard-boiled egg through a medium-mesh sieve to create egg "sprinkles."

4. To serve, arrange the leeks in heaps on plates and season with salt and pepper. Drizzle with vinaigrette and sprinkle with the egg and chervil. Serve immediately.

MAKING HARD-BOILED EGGS

Perfectly cooked hard-boiled eggs have a supple white and a creamy yolk. My preferred method is to place the eggs in a pan with cold water to cover, bring to a boil with the lid on, remove from the heat, and leave for 10 minutes in the hot water without disturbing. I then plunge the eggs in a bowl of ice water to stop the cooking and cool completely.

Cooled eggs are easier to peel than still-warm ones and it's preferable to use older eggs, as their membrane doesn't cling so tightly to the shell. Unpeeled hard-boiled eggs can be kept for 3 days in the refrigerator; peeled ones should be eaten within a day.

GARLIC ROSEMARY CROUTONS

Croûtons à l'ail et au romarin

MAKES 1½ CUPS /
85 G

**2 tablespoons
olive oil for cooking**

**½ teaspoon finely
chopped dried
rosemary**

**1 garlic clove,
pressed in a garlic
press or finely
chopped**

**2 cups / 85 g cubed
slightly stale, good-
quality baguette or
other French-style
loaf (cubes should
be ⅓ to ½ inch /
8 mm to 1 cm)**

**¼ teaspoon
fine sea salt**

**Freshly ground
black pepper**

As a typical Parisian, I buy a fresh baguette from the bakery once or twice a week. Which *boulangerie* I buy it from depends on where my errands are taking me and what day of the week it is; Paris bakeries close one or two days a week, but they have to consult with their nearby competitors so the neighborhood is never without a source of bread.

A good baguette keeps for a couple of days and fades quickly after that, becoming dry and a bit chewy, but I strive to use up those leftover pieces. I may whizz them in the food processor to make bread crumbs (see page 177), slice them and soak them in an eggy batter to make French toast (*pain perdu*, "lost bread"), or cube them to make these easy croutons.

Flavored with rosemary and garlic, the crisp and golden little cubes are meant to be sprinkled over soups and salads; I must warn you that if you start snacking on them, you may reach the bottom of the bowl sooner than you anticipated.

1. In a medium saucepan, combine the oil, rosemary, and garlic. Set over medium heat until the garlic and rosemary start to sizzle, about 1 minute. Remove from the heat and let rest for 10 minutes.

2. Preheat the oven to 350°F. / 175°C. and have ready a rimmed baking sheet.

3. Add the bread cubes and salt to the saucepan and stir to coat until no oil pools at the bottom of the pan.

4. Spread on the baking sheet and bake, stirring halfway through, until golden, about 10 minutes. Sprinkle with pepper and let cool. The croutons will keep for a week in an airtight container at room temperature.

2 tablespoons olive oil for cooking

1 small yellow onion (4¼ ounces / 120 g), finely sliced

1 medium butternut squash (2½-pounds / 1.2 kg), peeled and cubed

1 small / 700 g celery root, peeled and cubed

2 teaspoons fine sea salt

2 teaspoons finely chopped dried rosemary

4 cups / 1 liter Vegetable Stock (page 198), hot

Freshly ground black pepper

Heavy cream, for serving (optional)

Garlic Rosemary Croutons (page 111), for serving (optional)

BUTTERNUT AND CELERY ROOT SOUP

Velouté de courge butternut et céleri-rave

As enthusiastic as I am about a good winter squash soup, I find they can become cloying if one is not diligent about balancing their natural sweetness. In this soup, celery root is called to the rescue and its faint anise notes are most successful in lifting the flavors of the soup and steering them in a more subtle direction. It is a simple soup, and the only real work requested on your part is peeling the butternut squash (a vegetable peeler will do the job well) and the celery root (a slightly more involved task requiring a well-sharpened knife).

I like this soup on its own, with a crusty slice of sourdough bread, but if I'm serving it to friends I'll dress it up with a swirl of cream and a handful of Garlic Rosemary Croutons.

1. Heat the oil in a large soup pot. Add the onion and cook, stirring often, until softened, about 4 minutes. Stir in the squash, celery root, salt, and rosemary. Cook, stirring often, for 10 minutes.

2. Add the hot stock and pour in a little more hot water if needed to cover the vegetables. Bring to a simmer, cover, and cook over medium-low heat until the vegetables are soft, about 20 minutes.

3. Using a blender or an immersion blender, purée the soup until completely smooth. Taste and adjust the seasoning.

4. Reheat if necessary and ladle into bowls. Sprinkle with black pepper. Add a swirl of cream and serve with garlic rosemary croutons, if desired.

SHOCKING PINK PASTA
Pâtes rose vif

For this unusual and remarkably quick pasta dish, you simply blend raw beets together with cream, garlic, and a touch of cumin. This produces a shocking pink sauce that is perfect for tossing with cooked pasta—preferably long strands, such as spaghetti or bucatini—and crowning with fresh parsley and chopped almonds. If you want to push it up a notch in terms of sophistication, roast baby beets and cut them in quarters to garnish the pasta.

1. In a food processor or blender, combine the beets, cream, garlic, salt, and cumin. Process until smooth.

2. Bring salted water to a boil in a large pot. Add the pasta and cook until it's a minute shy of al dente. Drain, return the pasta to the pot, and fold in the sauce. Return to medium heat and cook until heated through and al dente, about 1 minute.

3. Divide among warm bowls, sprinkle with pepper, and top with the parsley and almonds. Serve immediately.

SERVES 4

12 ounces / 340 g beets, peeled and diced

1 cup / 240 ml light whipping cream or **unsweetened nondairy cream alternative**, such as soy or rice

1 garlic clove

1 teaspoon fine sea salt

1 teaspoon whole cumin seeds or **½ teaspoon ground cumin**

1 pound / 450 g long pasta, such as spaghetti, bucatini, or linguine

Freshly ground black pepper

1 cup / 20 g chopped fresh flat-leaf parsley leaves

⅔ cup / 85 g almonds, toasted (see page 68) and roughly chopped

PREHEATING PASTA BOWLS

To prevent pasta from cooling too quickly after serving, preheat the serving bowls or plates: a few minutes before your pasta is cooked, scoop a few tablespoons of the boiling pasta water into each bowl and set aside. Pour out the water just before serving; there's no need to dry the bowls.

2¼ pounds / 1 kg
mixed or brown
mushrooms

1 tablespoon olive oil
for cooking

1 small yellow onion
(4¼ ounces / 120 g),
finely chopped

1 medium / 125 g
carrot, peeled and
thinly sliced

1 stalk / 125 g celery,
thinly sliced

1 teaspoon
fine sea salt

¾ ounce / 20 g
dried mushrooms,
such as porcini
or shiitake

3 black peppercorns,
crushed with the side
of a chef's knife

½ teaspoon dried
thyme

1 bay leaf

Grated zest and juice
of 1 organic lemon

Parisian Gnocchi
(page 122),
refrigerated
and uncooked

Freshly ground
black pepper

Cold-pressed
hazelnut oil or
extra-virgin olive
oil, for drizzling

1 cup / 20 g fresh
flat-leaf parsley
leaves

MUSHROOM BROTH WITH PARISIAN GNOCCHI

Bouillon de champignons et gnocchi parisiens

Recipes often call for mushroom caps only, relegating the stems to the trash bin. Instead, I save the trimmings in a container in the freezer and, when I have enough, use them in this warming broth. Of course, you could use whole mushrooms, too, and if you have a mix of varieties your broth will be that much more aromatic.

This mushroom broth can be put to a great many uses. Here, I use it to poach gnocchi served in a bowl of the steaming broth with sliced mushrooms, a squeeze of lemon juice, and a bit of fresh parsley. I also use it as the base for vegetable and grain soups, with pearl barley for instance, which I cook in the broth itself, adding thinly sliced green cabbage a few minutes before serving.

1. Trim the mushrooms and set aside 7 ounces / 200 g whole mushroom caps, about 20 small ones. Chop the rest of the mushrooms and/or trimmings finely.

2. Heat the cooking olive oil in a large saucepan over medium heat. Add the chopped mushrooms, onion, carrot, celery, and salt, and cook, stirring often, until softened, about 4 minutes. Add the dried mushrooms, peppercorns, thyme, bay leaf, and lemon zest. Pour in 6 cups / 1.5 liters cold water. Cover, bring to a low simmer, and cook for 30 minutes.

RECIPE CONTINUES

3. Set a fine-mesh sieve over a large bowl and ladle the broth into the sieve to filter out the solids; discard the solids. Rinse the saucepan and pour the filtered broth back in. Taste and adjust the seasoning.

4. Bring to a low simmer and poach the gnocchi in the mushroom broth using the method described in the gnocchi recipe (see page 123). With a slotted spoon, divide the cooked gnocchi among 4 bowls.

5. Thinly slice the reserved mushroom caps and divide among the bowls.

6. Sprinkle each bowl with pepper, drizzle with hazelnut oil, squeeze in a little lemon juice, and add chopped parsley. Ladle the broth into the bowls at the table, pouring it against the sides to avoid disturbing the solids.

MUSHROOMS

Buy whole mushrooms with even-colored caps that show no signs of bruising and feel firm to the touch, not soft or damp. The stem should be firmly attached to the cap. Buy them loose if you can, so you can check that all of them look healthy; crates or boxes may have moldy specimens hiding at the bottom.

Store mushrooms in a paper bag in the refrigerator and use soon after purchasing. Just before using, brush them briefly with a soft brush or kitchen towel under a stream of cold water to remove the dirt. Avoid soaking; mushrooms absorb too much water.

CORSICAN TURNOVERS WITH WINTER SQUASH

Bastelles à la courge

Everywhere I turned in Corsica, my gaze fell on a table stacked with golden turnovers called *bastelles*, the dough folded up neatly like an envelope. Corsican cooks typically garnish them with *brocciu* (a ricotta-like sheep's milk cheese) and onions, along with fresh herbs or chard greens in the warmer months and winter squash in the fall.

Bastelles are traditionally made to celebrate All Saints' Day on the first day of November, and their preparation is a communal affair; the women gather into an assembly line to chop the onions, roll out the dough, and fold up the turnovers, destined for a wood-fired oven.

They make for a wonderful fall meal, served with a salad of mixed greens and fresh herbs dressed in Honey Lemon Vinaigrette (page 207). They're fun to make, all the elements can be prepared ahead, and there's no need to be too fussy with your folding technique; rustic is a good look on a bastelle.

1. Heat the oil in a large skillet over medium heat. Add the onions, garlic, and ½ teaspoon salt and cook, stirring often to prevent coloring, until soft, about 10 minutes.

2. Add the squash, rosemary, and ¾ teaspoon salt. Cover and cook, stirring often, until the squash is soft, 15 to 20 minutes. If the squash has released juices—this will depend on the variety—turn the heat up to high and cook for a few minutes longer, uncovered, until the juices have evaporated. Sprinkle with black pepper, then taste and adjust the seasoning. Set aside to cool.

RECIPE CONTINUES

SERVES 4

1 tablespoon olive oil for cooking

3 small red onions (4¼ ounces / 120 g each), minced

1 garlic clove, minced

Fine sea salt

1 small / 900 g red kuri, butternut, or kabocha squash, seeded, peeled, and diced

2 teaspoons finely chopped dried rosemary

Freshly ground black pepper

Olive Oil Tart Dough (page 200), made with the egg white and without the seeds

3. Preheat the oven to 400°F. / 200°C. and line a baking sheet with parchment paper.

4. Divide the dough into 4 equal pieces. On a lightly floured surface, roll out one of the pieces into an 8-inch / 20 cm square. Scoop one-fourth of the squash mixture onto the middle of the square. Bring two opposite corners of the dough into the center of the square and pinch them together. Lift the two remaining corners up to the center, matching the seams so they meet to form raised ridges. Crimp to seal. You'll get a square turnover, with ridges forming an "X" on top. Lift carefully with a spatula and transfer to the prepared baking sheet.

5. Repeat with the remaining dough and filling to form 3 more turnovers.

6. Bake, rotating the sheet in the oven halfway through cooking for even coloring, until golden, about 30 minutes. Let cool for 5 to 10 minutes before serving.

RED KURI SQUASH

Potimarron, aka Hokkaido squash or red kuri squash, is France's favorite winter squash. Shaped like a giant fig and roughly the size of a soccer ball, it has a smooth, bright orange skin. Its flesh doesn't fall apart when cooked, so it can be served in roasted chunks or used in warm salads, and its subtle chestnut flavor explains its name, a portmanteau of *potiron* (pumpkin) and *marron* (chestnut). The skin is thin, and if you buy organic, there's no need to peel it at all.

SERVES 4

1 cup / 240 ml
milk (not skim)
or unflavored,
unsweetened
nondairy milk

5 tablespoons /
65 g high-quality
unsalted butter,
diced

½ teaspoon
fine sea salt

1 cup / 130 g
all-purpose flour,
sifted

¼ teaspoon freshly
ground black pepper

Freshly grated
nutmeg

4 large organic eggs

PARISIAN GNOCCHI
Gnocchi parisiens

Parisian gnocchi may well be the least known use for choux pastry, yet it is one of my favorites. Most recipes using *pâte à choux* bake it in the oven so it puffs up; for Parisian gnocchi, you drop small pieces of the dough into a simmering liquid and poach them until they bob back to the surface, producing the tenderest little pillows imaginable. The one trick is to make sure you have all the ingredients measured out before you start cooking.

You can serve these gnocchi in a clear broth, such as on page 116. Once poached, you can also sauté them in sage butter until lightly browned and serve them over a bed of sautéed greens or other vegetables, or combine them with Béchamel Sauce (page 213) and grated cheese in a casserole to be baked into a golden gratin.

1. In a medium saucepan (not nonstick), combine the milk, butter, and salt and bring to a simmer over medium-low heat. Remove from the heat, add the flour all at once, and stir quickly with a wooden spoon until well blended and smooth. Return the pan to medium-low heat and keep stirring until the dough leaves a thin film at the bottom of the pan, indicating that the excess water has evaporated, about 3 minutes.

2. Let cool in the pan, off the heat, for 3 minutes. Add the pepper and a grating of nutmeg. Add the eggs one at a time, stirring well after each addition. When you first add an egg, it will seem as though the dough can't absorb it, but it will if you insist.

3. Transfer the dough to a sturdy freezer bag (to be used for piping the dough), press the air out, and zip or tie it shut. (You can also store the dough in a piping bag fitted with a ½-inch / 1 cm plain tip.) Refrigerate for 1 hour or up to a day.

4. Remove the freezer bag from the fridge and snip off one corner to create a ¾-inch / 2 cm opening.

5. To poach the gnocchi, bring salted water (or broth) to a low simmer in a large saucepan. Holding the bag close to the simmering water, press gently on the dough to force it out. As soon as it forms a small log about ½ inch / 1 cm in length, trim it off with a paring knife or kitchen shears so it falls into the water; be careful not to cause a splash and burn yourself. Repeat until you've used up all the dough; if you're not the most well-coordinated person on the planet, get an assistant to help you with the squeezing and snipping.

6. After 3 minutes, the gnocchi will rise back up to the surface, indicating they are done. A cooked gnocchi should feel bouncy between your fingers and will not taste like raw flour. Lift them out of the water with a slotted spoon. If you're still busy cutting fresh gnocchi into the pan when the first ones bob back up, you can leave them in for a short while; they won't suffer from an extra minute's cooking.

⅔ cup / 100 g
golden raisins

Olive oil for cooking

2 small yellow onions
(4¼ ounces / 120 g
each), minced

Fine sea salt

2 tablespoons
ras el hanout

1 pound / 450 g
small waxy potatoes

1 pound / 450 g thin
carrots, cut into
2-inch / 5 cm
segments

7 ounces / 200 g
small turnips,
quartered

4 stalks celery,
cut into ½-inch /
1 cm segments

2 quarts / 2 liters
Vegetable Stock
(page 198)

1 pound / 450 g
winter squash,
peeled and cut into
1-inch / 2.5 cm pieces

1 pound / 450 g
thin zucchini, cut into
2-inch / 5 cm
segments

2 cups / 320 g
cooked chickpeas
(from about ⅔ cup /
125 g dried)

Extra-virgin olive oil

COUSCOUS WITH VEGETABLES
Couscous aux légumes

Couscous is so deeply ingrained in France's culinary landscape that it is the nation's second favorite dish, between *blanquette de veau* (a creamy veal stew) and *moules-frites* (mussels with fries). Our colonial history and a century of rule in North Africa—for better or worse—has left us with a pronounced taste for this brothy stew served over fine wheat semolina.

The version that's served in restaurants is meat-heavy, featuring grilled lamb skewers, spicy sausages, stewed chicken, and sometimes all of the above, but my preference goes to vegetable couscous: a flavorsome stew of seasonal vegetables and chickpeas ladled over the steamed grain, and sprinkled with raisins and herbs.

This is a festive, communal dish that is conducive to stress-free entertaining, since the stew can be cooked in advance.

1. Soak the raisins in ½ cup / 120 ml hot water for 1 hour.

2. Heat 2 tablespoons cooking olive oil in a large stockpot over medium heat. Add the onions and ¼ teaspoon salt, and cook, stirring often to avoid coloring, until softened, about 4 minutes. Stir in the ras el hanout.

3. Add the potatoes, carrots, turnips, celery, and 1 teaspoon salt. Pour in the stock, cover, and bring to a simmer. Cook for 10 minutes at a low simmer.

4. Add the winter squash and zucchini and cook until all the vegetables are tender, about 15 minutes. Stir in two-thirds of the chickpeas and 2 tablespoons extra-virgin olive oil. (The dish may be prepared a day

RECIPE CONTINUES

3 cups / 550 g whole wheat couscous

3 cups / 720 ml boiling water

1 cup / 20 g chopped fresh flat-leaf parsley leaves

1 cup / 20 g chopped fresh cilantro leaves

Harissa, homemade (page 212) or store-bought

ahead up to this point. Cool completely, transfer to an airtight container, and refrigerate. The next day, reheat to just below simmering.)

5. Shortly before serving, place the couscous in a large heatproof bowl. Stir in 1½ teaspoons salt and 2 tablespoons extra-virgin olive oil. Pour the boiling water over the couscous, cover, and let stand for 10 minutes. Fluff the grains with a fork and transfer to a heated serving dish.

6. Combine the parsley and cilantro in a small serving bowl and place it on the table along with a bowl of the drained raisins, a bowl of the remaining chickpeas, and a ramekin of harissa. Ladle the vegetables and some of the broth onto plates of couscous and let your guests help themselves to the condiments.

RAS EL HANOUT

Ras el hanout is a complex mix of spices that enters into the preparation of many traditional North African dishes. It can include dozens of spices, but its composition depends on where you buy it; the name translates to "head of the shop," illustrating the pride that is taken in the secret formula that governs the making of this flagship item.

Bottled mixes sold outside of North Africa are often made with just a handful of spices, but an authentic ras el hanout will boast at least two dozen and up to fifty. If you're unable to find it, prepare a simplified version by grinding together equal amounts of cumin, cinnamon, coriander, ginger, nutmeg, black pepper, and turmeric.

ROLLED BARLEY AND CARROT STIR-FRY

Poêlée de flocons d'arge et carotte

An effortless way to increase the variety of grains you eat is to call upon the rolled grain, a multifaceted ingredient and all-around trouper: cheap, nutritious, and versatile. I am never without a bag or two or four of assorted *flocons de céréales*, as they're called in French, and I use them in many preparations, from granola to cookies, bread dough to fruit crumbles, and gratins to savory tarts.

I also like to make quick vegetable and grain stir-fries—*poêlées* in French—such as this one, where carrots and rolled barley are sautéed in a skillet until the barley becomes crisp and golden, with a satisfying chew. Garnished with fresh herbs and chopped walnuts, it is a tasty one-bowl meal that travels well if you want to take it to work for lunch. You can adapt the idea to any grain and vegetable you like: grated root vegetables or winter squash, minced winter greens, chopped mushrooms, or, come warmer days, peas, zucchini, or tomatoes.

1. In a medium bowl, combine the carrots, barley, onion, salt, curry powder, and sesame seeds. Stir in 1 cup / 240 ml water, cover, and refrigerate for 1 hour to allow the barley to plump.

2. Heat the 2 teaspoons cooking oil in a large skillet over medium heat. Add the barley mixture and cook, stirring from time to time, until the barley is golden and crisp in places, about 10 minutes.

3. Drizzle with extra-virgin olive oil, stir in the chervil and walnuts, and serve.

SERVES 4

2 medium / 250 g carrots, peeled and grated

2 cups / 200 g rolled barley, or other rolled grain

½ medium yellow onion (3 ounces / 85 g), finely chopped

1 teaspoon fine sea salt

1 teaspoon curry powder (substitute any spice mix you prefer)

2 tablespoons sesame seeds, toasted (see page 68)

2 teaspoons olive oil for cooking

Extra-virgin olive oil

1 cup / 20 g chopped fresh chervil or cilantro leaves

¾ cup / 75 g walnut halves, roughly chopped

6 burger-size
portobello
mushroom caps
(3½ ounces /
100 g each)

1¼ pounds / 560 g
brown mushrooms

Olive oil for cooking

Grated zest of
1 organic lemon

Fine sea salt

2 small red onions
(4¼ ounces / 120 g
each), minced

1 garlic clove,
finely chopped

10 ounces / 280 g
plums, pitted and
chopped

⅔ cup / 65 g
hazelnuts, toasted
(see page 68) and
roughly chopped

1 cup / 20 g fresh
chopped flat-leaf
parsley leaves

Freshly ground
black pepper

MUSHROOMS STUFFED WITH PLUMS AND HAZELNUTS

*Champignons farcis aux prunes
et aux noisettes*

There is something uniquely satisfying about mushrooms,
something almost meaty about the potency of their flavor and
the juiciness of their chewy texture. I am rather fond of stuffed
mushrooms and for that I use either brown mushrooms that are
on the bigger side or burger-size portobello mushrooms. This
fall filling is a satisfying mix of mushrooms, subtly sweet plums,
aromatic lemon zest, crunchy hazelnuts, and verdant parsley.
It is the kind of easy yet elegant dish that I'll serve to friends
coming over for dinner, with a side of Blanch-Roasted New
Potatoes (page 23), and no one ever asks where the meat is.

Plum season tapers out as we get deeper into the fall; if local
plums are no longer available when you make this, use cooking
apples instead.

1. Brush all the mushrooms gently with a damp towel to
   remove any trace of dirt; trim their stems as needed.
   Arrange the portobello mushroom caps, gill-side up,
   on a baking sheet. Drizzle with olive oil and sprinkle
   with the lemon zest and a little salt.

2. Cut the brown mushrooms into ½-inch / 1 cm dice.

3. Heat 1 tablespoon olive oil in a large skillet over
   medium heat. Add the onions, garlic, and ½ teaspoon
   salt. Cook, stirring often to avoid coloring, until softened, about 4 minutes. Add the diced mushrooms
   and ½ teaspoon salt, stir, and cook for 5 minutes. Add
   the chopped plums and cook until the mushrooms are

cooked through and the plums are very soft, about 5 minutes. Remove from the heat and stir in the hazelnuts and half of the parsley. (The filling can be made several hours ahead. Refrigerate in an airtight container.)

4. Preheat the oven to 400°F. / 200°C.

5. Divide the filling among the portobello caps and bake until heated through and slightly browned, 20 minutes.

6. Sprinkle the remaining parsley and some black pepper over the mushrooms and serve.

8 large Savoy
cabbage leaves, with
no holes or tears

2 ounces / 55 g
sorrel

4½ ounces / 130 g
spinach

4½ ounces / 130 g
Swiss chard

7 ounces / 200 g
leeks, white part
only, thinly sliced

1 cup / 20 g chopped
fresh flat-leaf parsley
leaves

3 large organic eggs

3 tablespoons crème
fraîche or sour cream

⅔ cup / 85 g
all-purpose flour

1½ teaspoons
fine sea salt

Freshly ground
black pepper

POITEVIN CABBAGE PARCELS
Farci poitevin

Farci poitevin is a traditional dish from the Poitou, a swampy, beautiful, and underexplored region in the West of France. It comprises cabbage leaves stuffed with an egg-and-cream batter made green by an abundance of edible leaves: sorrel, spinach, chard, parsley, but also radish tops, turnip leaves, lettuce, or any other green that's been growing increasingly impatient in the fridge.

Every Poitou family has its own recipe that it swears is the one and only true *farci poitevin*, but in all of them the cabbage leaves are held together by a special cloth netting and plunged into simmering stock to cook for a few hours. The finished dish is then sliced into wedges to be served warm or cold. As that netting is hard to find and not much easier to handle, I've transformed the process slightly: I either fold the cabbage leaves into individual stuffed parcels to be steamed, or assemble the dish in a loaf pan (or individual ramekins) lined with cabbage leaves to be baked in the oven.

Serve with the sharpest Dijon mustard you can find and a side of Potato and Celery Root Gratin (page 136).

1. Bring salted water to a boil in a medium saucepan. Working in batches, add the cabbage leaves and cook to soften, about 4 minutes. Rinse in cold water to stop the cooking, drain carefully and spread out on a kitchen towel to dry. Cut away the hard base of the center ribs so the leaves are pliable, but still offer enough surface area to hold the stuffing.

2. Remove the stems and center ribs of the sorrel, spinach, and Swiss chard and save for the stock box (see page 198) or other use. Make sure the leaves are dry. Gather

them into a pile, slice into ½-inch / 1 cm strips, and then slice the strips crosswise to form ½-inch / 1 cm squares.

3. In a large bowl, combine the chopped greens with the leeks and parsley. Add the eggs and crème fraîche and mix vigorously for a minute or two; the leaves will reduce in volume slightly. Add the flour and salt, season with pepper, and mix again.

TO MAKE INDIVIDUAL CABBAGE PARCELS

Take each cabbage leaf in turn and place it flat on your work surface. Spoon about one-eighth of the stuffing onto the center of the leaf. Gather the sides and ends of the leaf up and over it and secure the leaf into a parcel with one or two toothpicks.

Set up a large steamer. Arrange the filled parcels in the basket of the steamer and steam, tightly covered, for 1 hour (checking the water level from time to time). Serve warm.

TO BAKE INTO A LOAF (OR INDIVIDUAL RAMEKINS)

Preheat the oven to 350°F. / 175°C. and grease a small loaf pan or 6 ramekins.

Line the loaf pan or ramekins with the cabbage leaves in an overlapping pattern, leaving overhang at the top. Pour in the filling and fold the tops of the cabbage leaves back over it. Cover with foil and place the loaf pan (or ramekins) in a baking dish, and pour warm water into the dish so that it is half-full. Bake for 1½ hours. Cut the loaf into slices (or unmold the ramekins) and serve warm. Leftover slices can be sautéed in a skillet to reheat.

SERVES 4 TO 6

4 teaspoons olive oil for cooking, plus more for the pan

4½ pounds / 2 kg mixed root vegetables

1½ teaspoons fine sea salt

1½ teaspoons cumin seeds

¼ teaspoon cayenne pepper, or more to taste

Freshly ground black pepper

Gribiche Sauce (page 210)

ROASTED ROOTS WITH GRIBICHE SAUCE

Racines rôties, sauce gribiche

With the advent of fall comes the gorgeous family of root vegetables: carrots and potatoes, yes, but also beets, parsnips, rutabaga, parsley root, Jerusalem artichokes, celery root—all of them sweet and complex, their flavors subtle, and their flesh oh-so-satisfying.

A good roasting in the oven is the most efficient—and effortless—way to bring out the above qualities. All that's required is a nice colorful medley of varieties, cut into even-size pieces, and tossed together with oil and spices. In a little under an hour, the chunks are appetizingly browned and caramelized around the edges and they're ready to be enjoyed like the fall treat that they are, with or without a sauce. Herbed Tahini Sauce (page 214) makes a nice alternative to the gribiche sauce.

1. Preheat the oven to 400°F. / 200°C. and oil a rimmed baking sheet.

2. Trim and peel the root vegetables as needed; I usually leave the skin on potatoes (but brush them well) and young carrots. Cut the vegetables into sticks, about ¾ inch / 2 cm thick and 3 inches / 8 cm long. Depending on the initial shape of the vegetables, you won't get perfect sticks; just make the pieces uniform in thickness, so they'll cook at the same rate.

3. Transfer to the baking sheet, drizzle with the olive oil, and sprinkle with the salt, cumin, cayenne, and black pepper. Flip and stir the vegetables until evenly coated. Spread the vegetables on the baking sheet so they're

more or less in a single layer; they shouldn't be too crowded, or they will steam in their collective moisture and won't roast properly. Bake, flipping once or twice, until cooked through and appetizingly browned, 40 to 50 minutes.

4. Serve immediately with the gribiche sauce on the side.

SERVES 4 TO 6

½ cup / 100 g
brown rice

½ cup / 115 g French
green lentils

Fine sea salt

Freshly ground
black pepper

1⅔ pounds / 760 g
broccoli florets
(from a 2½-pound /
1 kg head)

⅓ cup / 80 ml
heavy cream or
unsweetened
nondairy cream

1 garlic clove,
finely chopped

Freshly grated
nutmeg

2 tablespoons plain
dried bread crumbs

Hot sauce, for
serving (optional)

BROCCOLI PARMENTIER
Parmentier de brocoli

Hachis parmentier is a traditional French dish of cooked ground meat, usually beef, baked under a thick blanket of mashed potatoes. (While elsewhere it may be known as "shepherd's pie," here it is named after Mr. Parmentier, the eighteenth-century French agronomist who popularized spuds for human consumption.) It is a thrifty preparation created to make use of leftovers; at the school cafeteria when I was growing up, roast beef day was unfailingly followed by hachis parmentier day.

Evolving from this classic recipe, *parmentier* has become a generic term for baked dishes topped with a layer of mashed vegetables. My favorite version is this one, with a mix of rice and lentils at the bottom and mashed broccoli on top. It makes for a comforting weeknight meal and all the ingredients but the cream can be kept on hand in the pantry or freezer.

1. Cook the brown rice and lentils in a large amount of unsalted boiling water, according to package directions. (Brown rice usually cooks in 30 to 45 minutes; lentils

BROCCOLI

Choose heads of broccoli with tightly bunched florets—they should resist if you try to pry them apart—and stems that feel firm, not limp. Most recipes call for florets only, but it is generally cheaper to buy whole heads and save the thick central stem. Peel off any part that's tough or browned and use the stems in broccoli soup, or grate them into a salad with raisins, sunflower seeds, and a yogurt dressing.

FRENCH GREEN LENTILS

The French love their lentils, and they have a preference for *lentilles vertes,* crocodile-green lentils that keep a slight al dente texture and don't turn to mush when cooked.

To cook green lentils, put them in twice their volume of cold, unsalted water. Cover, bring to a simmer, and cook until they reach the consistency you like, 15 to 30 minutes. As always when cooking legumes, don't salt the water until the last 5 minutes of cooking or the lentils will be tough. You can also season them after they're cooked.

in 15 to 30 minutes.) Drain if needed. Add ¾ teaspoon salt, sprinkle with black pepper, and stir to combine. Taste and adjust the seasoning. (This can be prepared up to a day ahead; cool, cover, and refrigerate.) Spread evenly in an 8-inch / 20 cm square baking dish.

2. Preheat the oven to 400°F. / 200°C.

3. Bring salted water to a boil in a large saucepan. Add the broccoli without crowding; you may have to work in two batches. Cover, return to a simmer, and cook until soft, 5 to 6 minutes.

4. Drain and transfer to a large bowl. Add the cream, garlic, and ¾ teaspoon salt and sprinkle with black pepper and nutmeg. Put the mixture through a potato ricer or food mill to get a smooth purée. Taste and adjust the seasoning.

5. Spread the broccoli purée in an even layer over the rice and lentils. Top with the bread crumbs and bake until heated through and lightly browned, 20 to 30 minutes. Serve immediately, with hot sauce, if desired.

1⅓ pounds / 600 g
yellow-fleshed
potatoes, such
as Yukon Gold

2 cups / 480 ml
milk (not skim, not
nondairy), plus
more as needed

1 garlic clove,
finely chopped

1½ teaspoons
fine sea salt

Freshly grated
nutmeg

1 small / 700 g
celery root

¼ cup / 60 ml
crème fraîche
or heavy cream

POTATO AND CELERY ROOT GRATIN

Gratin de pomme de terre et céleri-rave

Gratin dauphinois is a gloriously simple dish of sliced potatoes baked in milk, with a bit of cream and a murmur of nutmeg, until they develop an irresistible browned crusty top simply from the starch content, and without the crutch of cheese.

I make it frequently during the colder months, to present as a side or serve on its own with a salad. But over the years, my rendition has evolved into a two-flavor gratin that includes celery root in addition to the potatoes; the knobby root vegetable cooks to a consistency that is very close to that of spuds, brings a welcome flavor complexity, and makes the dish feel lighter.

The trick to a successful potato gratin is first to parboil the potatoes on the stove, until the milk thickens just enough to coat them well, and then finish baking the dish in the oven. This guarantees the potatoes are cooked through, top to bottom.

1. Scrub the potatoes, but don't peel them. With a sharp knife or mandoline slicer, cut the potatoes into ⅛-inch / 3 mm slices. Do not rinse after slicing.

2. In a medium saucepan, combine the potatoes, milk, garlic, salt, and a good grating of nutmeg. Bring to a simmer over medium-low heat and cook, stirring the potatoes and scraping the bottom of the pan regularly to prevent sticking, for 5 minutes. The milk will thicken to a creamy consistency; if you find the potatoes are absorbing most of the milk as they cook, add a little more to the pan. You should aim to have about ½ cup / 120 ml liquid in the pan after the potatoes have simmered for 5 minutes.

3. Preheat the oven to 425°F. / 220°C. and have ready a shallow earthenware or glass baking dish, about 2 quarts / 2 liters in capacity.

4. Peel the celery root, cut in wedges, and then into ⅛-inch / 3 mm slices. Be extra careful if you use a mandoline slicer, as celery root is tougher than potatoes.

5. Transfer one-third of the potatoes to the baking dish and top with half of the celery root. Dot with one-third of the crème fraîche. Top with another third of the potatoes and the remaining celery root. Dot with another third of the crème fraîche. Arrange the remaining potatoes on top, pour the milk from the saucepan all over them, and dot with the remaining crème fraîche.

6. Bake until bubbling at the edges and browned on top, 35 to 40 minutes. If the gratin is browning too quickly, cover loosely with foil and uncover for the final 5 minutes. Let stand for 5 to 10 minutes before serving.

7. You can bake the gratin a few hours ahead, cool, and reheat for 15 minutes in a 425°F. / 220°C. oven before serving.

CELERY ROOT

Celery root, also sold as celeriac or knob celery, is in season from late fall to early spring. It comes in gray-white heads, knobby and stringy, with a subtle flavor, sweet and earthy with notes of cumin and fennel. Choose small or medium heads that feel firm and heavy, with no darker spots or blemishes, and use within a week or two of purchasing.

SERVES 8

**Breton Shortbread
Tart Dough (page 45)**

**Grated zest of
1 organic orange**

**2 tablespoons
almond flour**

**1½ pounds / 680 g
fresh figs, quartered**

**1 tablespoon
unrefined blond cane
sugar (also sold as
evaporated cane
juice)**

EASY FRESH FIG TART
Tarte facile aux figues fraîches

Having grown up in Paris, I didn't encounter fig trees in the wild until my late twenties, when Maxence and I took a vacation on a small island in Croatia. Throughout the week, the official smell of our explorations was the peculiar scent of fig trees in the late summer heat, eerily sweet and reminiscent of coconut.

Every time I detected it, on a deserted road or a rocky trail, I would stop in my tracks and follow my nose to find the tree. If we were lucky, it would still be heavy with fruit, bursting with ripeness, a drop of syrupy sap pearling from their round bottoms.

I worried that these heavenly figs might spoil me forever, but no; I still derive immense pleasure from the baskets of French-grown figs I buy from late summer to early fall. And when "a platter of figs" doesn't feel like enough of a dessert for company, I make this fig tart. The flavor of the figs is flattered by a touch of orange zest and ground almonds and, as the fruit turns almost jam-like, it melds into the buttery crust that supports it.

1. Press the dough into an ungreased 10- to 12-inch / 25 to 30 cm tart pan with a removable bottom, cover loosely with plastic wrap, and refrigerate for 2 hours or overnight.

2. Preheat the oven to 350°F. / 175°C.

3. Sprinkle the crust with the orange zest and almond flour and arrange the quartered figs on top in a circular pattern, starting from the center. Sprinkle with the sugar. Bake until the crust is set and golden brown and the figs are thoroughly cooked, 40 to 50 minutes.

4. Run a knife around the pan to loosen, remove the sides, and let the tart cool completely before serving.

APPLE AND SALTED CARAMEL SAUCE

Sauce au caramel salé et à la pomme

This caramel sauce makes a fine companion to crêpes, yogurt, and baked or fresh fruit. The subtle tang of apple cider brings a lovely balance to the flavors, but other fruit juices can be used—orange juice in particular.

Unrefined sugar contains impurities that prevent it from caramelizing properly, so I revert to regular white sugar here.

MAKES ¹⁄₃ CUP / 80 ML

½ cup / 120 ml apple cider, hard cider, or natural unfiltered apple juice

3 tablespoons / 40 g granulated white sugar (not unrefined)

1 teaspoon cornstarch

2 tablespoons / 25 g unsalted butter or all-natural unsweetened almond butter

¼ teaspoon fine sea salt

1. Heat the apple cider in a saucepan until just below the simmering point.

2. Meanwhile, put the sugar (make sure it is lump-free) in a small saucepan over medium-low heat. Let the sugar melt; you can swirl the pan around, but do not stir.

3. Once the sugar is entirely melted, it will quickly take on a light amber color; remove the pan from the heat then. Wearing long sleeves and an oven mitt, pour in the hot cider with caution; it will spit and splatter and the caramel will harden. Return the pan over medium heat and stir until the caramel is melted again.

4. Put the cornstarch in a small heatproof bowl and whisk in 2 tablespoons of the caramel until dissolved. Pour back into the pan and whisk over medium heat as the mixture thickens slightly.

5. Remove from the heat and whisk in the butter and salt.

6. Serve immediately or at room temperature. Pour leftovers into a jar, refrigerate, and use within a few days.

2½ ounces / 70 g
plump pitted **prunes**,
very finely chopped

½ cup / 70 g whole
almonds, very finely
chopped

2 tablespoons **honey**

1 tablespoon
unsalted **butter**,
softened, or all-
natural unsweetened
almond butter

A good pinch of
fine sea salt

6 small mildly tart
organic **baking
apples**

¼ cup / 60 ml **apple
cider, hard cider, or
natural unfiltered
apple juice**

BAKED APPLES WITH PRUNES AND ALMONDS

Pommes en chemise, pruneaux et amandes

I take a special delight in the imaginative naming of some
French dishes and this is one of them: whole apples baked in
their skins (unpeeled) are called *pommes en chemise*, or apples
with their shirts on. Isn't that poetic? But really, the fondness
I have for baked apples extends beyond the name; they are
an easily prepared, comforting, and delicious dessert to make
during the cold months, one that fills the house with a promising
smell and is always well received.

Jonagold, Gala, and Braeburn apples are good choices, but
try lesser-known, local varieties, too. I stuff the cores with a mix
of prunes and almonds, but any dried fruit and nut combo will
do; use what you have on hand. For serving, a good vanilla ice
cream will never fail you, but consider making your own Apple
and Salted Caramel Sauce (page 139) and adding a little crème
fraîche or Greek yogurt.

1. Preheat the oven to 325°F. / 160°C.

2. In a small bowl, stir together the prunes, almonds,
   honey, butter, and salt to form a paste.

3. Slice "hats" off the tops of the apples. Core the
   apples with an apple corer or a sharp paring knife.
   Arrange the apples in a baking dish large enough to
   accommodate them without crowding.

4. Fill the core of each apple with the stuffing, packing it
   as tightly as you can. Place the hats back on the apples.
   Pour the apple cider into the bottom of the dish and
   cover loosely with foil.

5. Bake, basting the apples with the cider every 15 to 20 minutes, until the flesh is cooked through and the skin puffy, 40 minutes to 1 hour, depending on the size and variety of the apples.

6. Let cool for 10 minutes before serving.

PEAR AND CHESTNUT CAKE
Fondant poire et châtaigne

I fell in love with chestnut flour during a vacation in Corsica, where chestnut trees flourish on the steep slopes of the mountains in the heart of the island. The fruits of these trees are eaten as is or turned into a velvety jam, but a good portion is also dried, hulled, and milled into a fine off-white powder that boasts a one-of-a-kind flavor, earthy and sweet.

Driving up narrow, bumpy roads through chestnut groves that summer, we stopped for lunch in Evisa, a village so pretty it hurt, and at the local *épicerie* I bought two kilos of chestnut flour to experiment with.

This pear and chestnut cake is among my proudest successes. It is moist-crumbed, with tender chunks of fruit, and the crystals of sanding sugar sprinkled on top create an irresistible, finely crisp layer.

1. Preheat the oven to 350°F. / 175°C. Line the bottom of a 10-inch / 25 cm cake pan with parchment paper and grease the sides.

2. In a medium bowl, beat together the cane sugar and the eggs. Add the yogurt and oil and beat until combined.

3. In a second bowl, combine the flours, salt, baking powder, and baking soda, stirring with a whisk to remove any lumps.

4. Fold the flour mixture and diced pears into the yogurt mixture until no trace of flour remains. The batter will be thick; avoid overworking it.

RECIPE CONTINUES

SERVES 10

⅓ cup / 80 ml olive oil for cooking, plus more for the pan

¾ cup plus 2 tablespoons / 200 g blond unrefined cane sugar (also sold as evaporated cane juice)

2 large organic eggs

1 cup / 240 ml plain all-natural yogurt

⅔ cup / 85 g chestnut flour

1 cup plus 1 tablespoon / 140 g all-purpose flour

1 teaspoon fine sea salt

1½ teaspoons baking powder

½ teaspoon baking soda

1⅓ pounds / 600 g pears, cored and diced (unpeeled if organic)

2 tablespoons sanding sugar, for sprinkling

5. Pour into the prepared pan and level the surface with a spatula. Sprinkle the sanding sugar across the surface. Bake until the top is golden brown and a knife inserted in the middle of the cake comes out clean, 40 minutes.

6. Let cool in the pan for 1 hour and then transfer to a rack to cool completely before serving.

pantry gem

CHESTNUT FLOUR

Chestnut flour pairs well with fall and winter fruits such as oranges, apples, plums, and pears. Because it is an assertive flour, and pricier than most, it is generally used in combination with milder and cheaper flours in bread doughs and cake and cookie batters or to make chestnut crêpes as they do in Corsica.

Chestnut flour is available wherever chestnuts are grown, as well as online and in gourmet food stores, imported from France or Italy. Until you find it, you can substitute any other kind of alternative flour that will contribute interesting notes, such as buckwheat, rye, or spelt flour.

OLD-FASHIONED WALNUT AND CHOCOLATE MACARONS

Macarons à l'ancienne aux noix et au chocolat

MAKES 35 TO 40 BITE-SIZE SANDWICH COOKIES

½ cup plus 2 tablespoons / 125 g unrefined blond cane sugar (also sold as evaporated cane juice)

⅔ cup / 85 g walnuts, hazelnuts, or pecans

½ cup / 70 g almonds, blanched or not (or ⅔ cup / 85 g almond flour)

2 large organic egg whites

¼ teaspoon fine sea salt

2 ounces / 55 g good-quality bittersweet chocolate (about 65% cacao)

The French word *macaron* has been recently popularized by the craze over the Parisian macaron, a fancy and fragile confection that comes in all colors of the rainbow—sometimes worryingly so—and any flavor you could possibly imagine.

Few people know that this particular macaron is a fairly novel invention, and just one of many macarons that have been eaten in France since the seventeenth century. Although there are many regional variations of the little cookies, the basic premise is the same: All are made from ground almonds, sugar, and egg whites, with the occasional addition of honey, bitter almond extract, or some other ingredient kept secret for generations.

Tan or golden, with a crisp exterior and a moist, chewy heart, these old-fashioned macarons are a little bit rustic and infinitely more endearing to me than their splashy Parisian counterparts. I prepare mine with a combination of ground almonds and walnuts and assemble them two by two with a dollop of melted dark chocolate. An absolute treat with a cup of tea or coffee, they may be wrapped up prettily and given away as an edible gift, too.

1. Preheat the oven to 350°F. / 175°C and line a baking sheet with parchment paper.

2. In a blender or food processor, process the sugar, walnuts, and almonds (if you're using almond flour, leave it out) in short pulses until finely ground. Don't process continuously or the nuts may release their oil.

RECIPE CONTINUES

Transfer to a medium bowl (if you're using almond flour, add it now and stir to combine and remove any lumps).

3. In a separate bowl, combine the egg whites, 1 tablespoon cold water, and the salt. Using a whisk or an electric mixer, beat the egg whites until they form soft peaks. Fold the egg whites into the dry ingredients with a spatula, lifting the mixture gently to avoid deflating.

4. Transfer to a piping bag fitted with a plain ½-inch / 1 cm tip. (Alternatively, use a sturdy freezer bag and snip off one corner to create a ¾-inch / 2 cm opening.)

5. Pipe a small dot of batter under each corner of the parchment paper so it will stay in place as you pipe. Pipe small round mounds of batter onto the parchment paper, each about 1 inch / 2.5 cm in diameter, leaving about 1 inch / 2.5 cm of space between them. Strive to make them even in size; you should get 70 to 80 mounds in total. Using a pastry brush or the back of a spoon lightly dipped in water, pat the surface to smooth down the pointy tip you've formed while piping.

6. Bake until golden on top and lightly browned around the edges, 10 to 12 minutes.

7. Lift the parchment paper cautiously by each of the corners in turn and spray cold water underneath. Let rest for 2 minutes—the steam will help release the macarons—and then transfer the cookies with a thin spatula to a cooling rack. Cool completely.

8. Melt the chocolate in a double boiler (see page 51). It should be creamy, not runny; let cool slightly if needed.

9. It is likely that your macaron halves won't be perfectly even in size; find a same-size buddy for each of them and group them in pairs on the cooling rack.

10. Pick up a macaron half, spoon a dollop of chocolate on its flat side, and top with the matching half. Return to the cooling rack. Repeat with the remaining macaron halves. Let rest for 2 hours or until the chocolate is set.

11. The macarons will keep for a few days at room temperature in an airtight container.

WINTER

L' hiver

The holidays are tremendous occasions in France, with families gathering for Christmas celebrations and friends getting together to usher in the New Year. In both cases, food is the guest of honor. And although roasted and stuffed birds are classic centerpieces on holiday tables, you'll see that it is absolutely possible to create a meatless French-style spread that feels just as celebratory as the expected one.

This chapter also offers inspiration for vegetarian dishes that are a delight to come home to on a winter night. Hearty and wholesome enough to keep you satisfied, they still provide the freshness of taste that is so hard to find in wintry cooking.

PRODUCE TO PLAY WITH IN THE WINTER

• Apples	• Celery root	• Kumquats	• Oranges	• Shallots
• Beets	• Endives	• Leeks	• Parsnips	• Spinach
• Brussels sprouts	• Garlic	• Lemons	• Pears	• Tangerines
• Cabbage	• Grapefruit	• Mâche	• Persimmons	• Turnips
• Carrots	• Jerusalem artichokes	• Mushrooms	• Potatoes	• Walnuts
• Cauliflower	• Kiwifruit	• Onions	• Salsify	• Winter squash

JERUSALEM ARTICHOKE AND POTATO CANAPÉS

Canapés de pomme de terre au topinambour

Jerusalem artichokes are a typical example of what the French call *légumes oubliés,* or forgotten vegetables. This umbrella term includes not only heirloom varieties that have fallen by the wayside in favor of hardier, glossier ones, but also those vegetables our grandparents resorted to eating during World War II, in spite of their cattle fodder status, because the more palatable options were commandeered and rationed. These were swiftly "forgotten" after the war, because of the bad memories they conjured.

But the Jerusalem artichoke (or sunchoke) is now back in style and that's a very good thing, as it is a truly delicious vegetable with a distinctive artichoke-like flavor. It can be cooked, taking on a creamy texture similar to that of baking potatoes, but it can also be eaten raw, either grated or sliced.

These canapés are built on slices of potato and topped with a quick salad of paper-thin sunchoke slices dressed with hazelnut oil to accent their nuttiness. Add a little dill on top, and you have an attractive winter nibble to serve at a holiday buffet or with predinner drinks.

MAKES ABOUT
25 CANAPÉS

14 ounces / 400 g small waxy **potatoes** (each about 1½ inches / 4 cm in diameter), different colors if possible

1 teaspoon **cider vinegar**

1 teaspoon **freshly squeezed lemon juice**

1 teaspoon **cold-pressed hazelnut oil** or **walnut oil** or **untoasted sesame oil**

1 teaspoon **extra-virgin olive oil**

3½ ounces / 100 g thin **Jerusalem artichokes**

Fleur de sel or other flaky sea salt

Freshly ground black pepper

⅓ cup / 80 ml **crème fraîche**, **sour cream**, or all-natural **Greek yogurt**

A few sprigs of **dill**

1. Keep the skin on the potatoes if it's thin. Cut the potatoes into ⅓-inch / 8 mm slices. Set up a steamer. Steam the potatoes, tightly covered, until cooked through, 10 to 12 minutes. Let cool completely.

2. In a bowl, whisk together the vinegar, lemon juice, and oils.

RECIPE CONTINUES

JERUSALEM ARTICHOKES

Look for Jerusalem artichokes, sometimes labeled as sunchokes or sunroots, at farmers' markets or well-stocked grocery stores. These small, pink- or beige-skinned root vegetables appear in late fall and stick around until March or April. It is normal for their skin to be a bit coarse, but it shouldn't appear overly thick or wrinkled, and their flesh should be firm. Depending on the variety, Jerusalem artichokes may have stubs and bulges; for easier peeling, the fewer the better.

3. Peel the Jerusalem artichokes and rinse them well. Leave them whole if they are thin; otherwise quarter them lengthwise, so they'll produce small slices. Using a mandoline slicer or very sharp knife, cut into paper-thin slices or thin matchsticks. Toss in the dressing as you go to minimize oxidation. Sprinkle with salt and pepper, then taste and adjust the seasoning.

4. Arrange the potato slices on a serving plate, dab each with a little crème fraîche, and sprinkle with salt. Using your fingers, plop a mound of Jerusalem artichoke slices on each potato slice. Top with a tuft of dill, sprinkle with pepper, and serve.

pantry gem

HAZELNUT OIL

You'll find hazelnut oil at gourmet grocery stores and natural foods stores. Like most nut oils, it is not cheap, but so vivid in flavor that only a small amount is needed as a finishing oil, drizzled over roasted butternut squash, zucchini pasta, or in the Very Green Salad on page 18.

ASSORTED SAVORY PUFFS
Gougères assorties

I will never tire of the magic of *pâte à choux,* or choux pastry. I love how this basic mix of butter, milk, flour, and eggs puffs up so appealingly in the oven, creating such an irresistible texture—the crisp shell giving way to a moist and tender interior.

My most frequent use for it is gougères, savory bite-size puffs, often flavored with cheese, to serve with a predinner glass of wine. I have become fond of making assorted gougères: I divide the dough into three parts, flavor one with Comté cheese, another with chopped parsley, and the last with cumin. Three flavors are so much better than one and no more difficult to prepare.

1. In a medium saucepan (not nonstick), combine the butter, salt, and milk and bring to a simmer over medium-low heat. Remove from the heat, add the flour all at once, and stir quickly with a wooden spoon until well blended and smooth. Return the pan to medium-low heat and keep stirring until the dough leaves a thin film at the bottom of the pan, indicating that the excess water has evaporated, about 3 minutes.

2. Let cool in the pan, off the heat, for 3 minutes. Add the pepper and a generous grating of nutmeg. Add the eggs one at a time, stirring well after each addition. When you first add an egg, it will seem as though the dough can't absorb it, but it will if you insist.

3. Divide the dough in three equal parts; each should weigh about 7 ounces / 200 g. Fold the grated cheese into the first, the parsley into the second, and the cumin seeds into the third. Scoop each into a small but

RECIPE CONTINUES

MAKES ABOUT 60
BITE-SIZE PUFFS

5 tablespoons / 70 g high-quality unsalted butter, diced

½ teaspoon fine sea salt

1 cup / 240 ml milk (not skim) or unflavored, unsweetened nondairy milk

1 cup / 130 g all-purpose flour, sifted

¼ teaspoon freshly ground black pepper

Freshly grated nutmeg

4 large organic eggs

½ cup / 40 g freshly and finely grated Comté or Gruyère cheese

½ cup / 20 g very finely chopped fresh flat-leaf parsley leaves

¾ teaspoon cumin seeds, toasted (see page 68), or ½ teaspoon ground cumin

sturdy freezer bag (to be used for piping the dough), press the air out, and zip or tie it shut. (This can be prepared in advance; refrigerate for up to a day, and remove from the fridge 1 hour before baking.)

4. Preheat the oven to 400°F. / 200°C. and line a baking sheet with parchment paper.

5. Snip off one corner of one freezer bag to create a ¾-inch / 2 cm opening, and pipe a small dot of dough under each corner of the parchment paper so it will stay in place as you pipe. Pipe small round mounds of dough onto the parchment paper, each about 1 inch / 2.5 cm in diameter, leaving about 1 inch / 2.5 cm of space between them. Using a pastry brush or the back of a spoon lightly dipped in water, pat the surface of the mounds gently to smooth.

6. Repeat with the other two freezer bags; you will likely have to work in batches.

7. Bake, without opening the oven door during the first 10 minutes, until puffed and golden, 15 to 20 minutes. Make sure the sides of the puffs are golden, too, or they will soften as they cool. Transfer to a cooling rack. Serve warm or at room temperature.

note Once the puffs have been baked and cooled, you can freeze them in a container or freezer bag. Pop them back into a 400°F. / 200°C. oven for 5 minutes; there's no need to thaw them first.

SERVES 4 TO 6

1 cup / 185 g
uncooked medium
bulgur

2 cups / 480 ml
boiling water

3 medium / 375 g
carrots, peeled and
grated

2 medium / 340 g
beets, peeled and
grated

3 good-quality
plump dried figs,
finely diced

½ cup / 60 g
cashews, toasted
(see page 68) and
roughly chopped

1 cup / 20 g chopped
fresh flat-leaf parsley
leaves

2 tablespoons
freshly squeezed
lemon juice

2 tablespoons
cider vinegar

1 teaspoon fine
sea salt

3 tablespoons
extra-virgin olive oil

Freshly ground
black pepper

Hot sauce

GRATED CARROT AND BEET SALAD WITH BULGUR AND FIGS
Salade de carottes et betteraves râpées, boulgour et figues

Because I work from home most of the time and eat lunch a few steps from my desk, preparing something refreshing for myself is a good way of taking a break and relaxing in the middle of the day.

Over the years, I have developed a few standbys, among them this no-cook winter salad of raw beets and carrots, grated into a large heap and joined by bulgur, dried figs, parsley, and cashews.

I recommend grating the carrots and beets on the large holes of your grater. In about the same amount of time it would take you to get out the food processor and later clean it, you can get a nice arm workout instead.

This is the rare salad that, stored in the refrigerator, will not only keep but actually improve over a couple of days.

1. In a heatproof bowl or pan, combine the bulgur and boiling water. Cover and let stand until tender, about 20 minutes. Drain well and let cool.

2. In a large salad bowl, combine the bulgur, carrots, beets, figs, cashews, and parsley. In a small bowl, combine the lemon juice, vinegar, and salt. Whisk in the olive oil and then pour over the salad ingredients. Sprinkle with black pepper and hot sauce, to taste, and then stir until thoroughly combined. Taste and adjust the seasoning.

BULGUR

Bulgur is made of precooked, ground dried wheat berries. It is widely used in Middle Eastern cuisines and around the Mediterranean rim, as a side or an ingredient in salads, soups, stuffings, and vegetable dishes to make them more filling. Because the grain has already been cooked when you buy it, bulgur can be ready in a short time—after a brief soaking or boiling step—and this makes it the impatient cook's best friend. You will find bulgur (possibly spelled bulgar, bulghur, burghul . . .) at natural foods stores and Middle Eastern markets.

FRENCH ENDIVE, ORANGE, AND WALNUT SALAD

Salade d'endives à l'orange et aux noix

French endive (also sold as Belgian endive) is a small leafy vegetable grown underneath a dome of soil to protect it from the light and thus prevent it from turning green. It can then be harvested all winter long and is quite popular in Belgium and in the North of France, where it goes by the name *chicon*.

Although endives can be cooked—most iconically wrapped in ham and baked in béchamel sauce for *endives au jambon*—it is raw that I like them best. Their refreshing crispness and subtle bitter notes make them ideal for quickly assembled winter salads such as this one, which pairs them with walnuts and oranges and is so good I've successfully used it to convert friends who thought they didn't like endives. The recipe may be doubled for a crowd, and if you wish to make it more substantial, it is very good with cooked and cooled lentils added to it.

1. Segment the oranges (see page 160) over a medium salad bowl to collect the juices; set the segments aside.

2. Add the honey, mustard, and salt to the bowl and stir until smooth. Whisk in the olive oil.

3. Cut the endives lengthwise into quarters, carve out and discard the core, and cut the leaves crosswise into ½-inch / 1 cm slices, leaving the delicate tips whole. Add to the bowl and toss to coat.

4. Add the orange segments and walnuts and toss to combine. Serve immediately or let sit for up to 1 hour.

RECIPE CONTINUES

SERVES 4

2 medium oranges

2 teaspoons mild honey

1 teaspoon Dijon mustard

½ teaspoon fine sea salt

3 tablespoons extra-virgin olive oil

1⅓ pounds / 600 g French endives

1 cup / 100 g walnut halves, toasted (see page 68) and roughly chopped

FRENCH ENDIVES

French endives (also marketed as Belgian endives) look like torpedo-shaped lettuce hearts, about as big as a hand, with smooth, cream-colored leaves and slightly ruffled yellow-green tips. They are not to be confused with another type of endive, which may also be sold as curly endive, chicory, or frisée, that comes in light green, frilly salad leaves. When choosing French endives, make sure they are firm and their leaves unblemished and tightly bundled; if they feel loose and soft at your gentle squeeze, they've been picked too long ago.

SEGMENTING AN ORANGE

Segmenting (or supreming) an orange means cutting it into pretty, flesh-only segments, with no peel, pith, or membranes. It takes a little practice, but you won't regret developing the skill; the resulting segments burst into juice as you bite them and they make handsome additions to desserts and salads.

With a well-sharpened knife, slice off the top and bottom of the orange horizontally, cutting off just enough so that the flesh is exposed. With the fruit resting on the cutting board on one of its now-flat ends, slice off a strip of peel from the top edge to the bottom, working the blade along the curve of the orange to remove the peel and white pith along with the thinnest sliver of flesh possible. Repeat until you've rid the fruit of all its peel.

You can now make out the segments, separated by a thin white membrane. Holding the orange in one hand, slice into the orange vertically, inserting the blade of a paring knife as closely as possible along one membrane wall, until you reach the core. Make a similar cut on the opposite side of the wedge you've started to loosen to extract the segment. Repeat until you've cut out all the segments.

ROASTED BEET SOUP WITH BABY SPINACH AND SQUASH SEED PESTO

Velouté de betterave rôtie, pistou de pousses d'épinard et graines de courge

SERVES 4 TO 6

2 pounds / 900 g small or medium red beets, evenly sized

2½ ounces / 70 g baby spinach leaves (about 4 cups)

¼ cup / 40 g hulled pumpkin seeds, toasted (see page 68)

¼ cup / 60 ml extra-virgin olive oil, plus more as needed

1 garlic clove

Fine sea salt

Freshly ground black pepper

4 cups / 1 liter Vegetable Stock (page 198)

2 teaspoons ground cumin

Roasting beets transforms them in a way no other cooking method does, bringing out their sweetness, but also a hint of smoke from their skin's exposure to high heat. Once peeled, roasted beets may enter into myriad preparations. Blitzing them into a soup with homemade vegetable stock is a particularly gratifying endeavor; their flavor can then shine through in a dramatic purple *velouté,* the French word for a puréed soup, evoking its velvety consistency.

While beet fans may be content to drink it up like a smoothie, I usually serve this soup with a quickly made parsley and squash seed *pistou,* the Provençal pesto, which provides a lightly nubby texture and accents the flavors of the soup nicely.

1. Scrub the beets but do not peel. Put them in a baking dish large enough to accommodate them comfortably.

2. Place in a cold oven and turn it to 475°F. / 250°C. Roast until a knife can be easily inserted into the center of the beets, 1 to 1½ hours depending on their size. Let rest until cool enough to handle, then peel and cut into chunks.

3. While the beets are roasting, prepare the pesto: In a blender or food processor, combine the spinach,

RECIPE CONTINUES

pumpkin seeds, oil, garlic, ½ teaspoon salt, and a generous grinding of pepper. Process until smooth, adding more oil as needed to reach your preferred consistency. Taste and adjust the seasoning.

4. In a blender, or in a medium soup pot if you're going to use an immersion blender, combine the beets, stock, cumin, and ½ teaspoon salt. Process until smooth and velvety; wear an apron and watch out for any splatter.

5. Reheat over medium-low heat, taste, and adjust the seasoning. Serve warm, topped with the pesto.

pantry gem

BEETS

Like most root vegetables, beets are harvested before the first frost and kept in storage for the duration of winter. Early-season beets are sold in bunches, with their leaves still on, and these you can handle like you would chard greens, spinach, or radish tops (see Radish-Top Pasta on page 26). Later in the year, beets are sold sans greens and it becomes necessary to check that they feel firm and smooth, rather than soft or wrinkled.

Beets are classically eaten cooked—boiled, steamed, or roasted—but don't overlook their potential as a raw vegetable, grated or very thinly sliced. Unless you're using golden beets, the flesh and juice can stain your clothes and skin, so handle them carefully.

SERVES 4

3 pounds / 1.4 kg leeks, trimmed

1 tablespoon olive oil for cooking, plus more for the pan

½ teaspoon fine sea salt

1 teaspoon curry powder

5 ounces / 140 g fresh goat cheese, cold from the fridge, cut into thin slices

Freshly ground black pepper

Yogurt Tart Dough (page 199)

½ cup / 20 g finely chopped fresh chives

CURRIED LEEK TART TATIN

Tatin de poireaux au curry

Beyond the original apple tart, baked upside down with the fruit at the bottom and the dough on top, the *tarte tatin* format can be applied to all manner of fillings, sweet or savory, and it is most flattering to vegetables that might otherwise dry out in the oven. This makes it well suited to leeks, which fare best in a moist environment, and are encouraged to soften under the protective mantle of the tart crust. The leek segments also look quite pretty, sitting upright in concentric circles, once the tart is flipped crust-side down.

I cook the leeks in a skillet first, to initiate the browning, and season them with curry powder, which is a perfect complement to their natural sweetness. I use a very flavorful curry powder called Kari Gosse, developed by a Breton apothecary in the early nineteenth century, when ships from the Far East still docked in local ports to unload their treasured spices. Use whichever curry powder you like, as long as it tastes fresh and not dusty.

1. Slice the leek whites into ¾-inch / 2 cm lengths. Put them in a bowl of cold water and swoosh them around gently to remove any sand or dirt, but keep the sections whole. Drain well.

2. Heat the olive oil in a large skillet over medium heat. Add the leeks, placing them cut-sides down and in a single layer. Sprinkle with the salt and curry powder, cover, and reduce the heat to medium-low. Cook for 10 minutes without disturbing, checking regularly that the leeks don't brown too much underneath; reduce the heat if they do. Let cool to room temperature.

3. Preheat the oven to 350°F. / 175°C.

4. Grease a 10-inch / 25 cm cake or tart pan with olive oil and arrange the leeks browned side up (the other side will brown while the tart bakes) in the pan in a single, tightly packed layer, leaving a ¾-inch / 2 cm margin all around. Top evenly with the goat cheese and sprinkle with pepper.

5. Roll out the dough between two sheets of parchment paper into a 12-inch / 30 cm round. Remove the top sheet of paper and, placing your hand underneath the dough, flip it onto the pan so it lands more or less centered over the ingredients; adjust if necessary. Remove the parchment paper, tuck the dough into the pan around the leeks, and pierce 3 to 4 holes in the top of the dough to make steam vents.

6. Bake until golden brown, 35 to 40 minutes. Run a knife around the crust to loosen and, holding the pan with oven mitts, invert it onto a serving plate. Any piece of leek that remains stuck to the pan can be placed back on the tart where it belongs.

7. Sprinkle with pepper and chives and serve.

LEEKS

Pick firm leeks that are on the thinner side, with as long a white part as possible and an outer layer that feels smooth and fresh, rather than parched or wrinkled. Check the color of the leaves; they should be a vibrant emerald green with no discoloration.

Because leeks are grown in sandy soil, they can hoard sand and dirt between their layers, so you should clean them carefully.

½ recipe **Buckwheat Pasta Dough** (page 202)

Cornmeal, for sprinkling

2 teaspoons olive oil for cooking

½ **medium yellow onion** (3 ounces / 85 g), finely sliced

1 garlic clove, minced

Fine sea salt

1¼ pounds / 560 g **Brussels sprouts**, thinly sliced

1 cup / 130 g **cooked shelled chestnuts**, diced (optional)

Freshly ground black pepper

3 tablespoons **extra-virgin olive oil**

Grated zest of 1 **organic lemon**

2 tablespoons **freshly squeezed lemon juice**

Parmesan or other hard cheese, cut into shavings (optional)

BUCKWHEAT AND BRUSSELS SPROUTS OPEN RAVIOLI
Ravioles ouvertes sarrasin et choux de Bruxelles

I was introduced to *ravioles ouvertes,* or open ravioli, while dining at one of Michelin three-star chef Anne-Sophie Pic's restaurants in Valence. Instead of painstakingly assembling ravioli pockets, and holding your breath when you cook them for fear they will spill their contents into the boiling water, this offers a simpler, conceptual take on the ravioli: little piles of filling mounded on the plate and a single piece of pasta dough draped over each to simulate ravioli tops.

In this version, I opt for thinly sliced and sautéed Brussels sprouts topped with squares of buckwheat pasta—inspired by *crozets,* tiny squares of buckwheat pasta popular in the Savoy region—and drizzle everything with a lemony olive oil. It makes for an elegant and delicious starter fit for a holiday meal. If you prefer, you are welcome to cut the pasta dough into tagliatelle and simply toss them with the Brussels sprouts and lemon oil.

1. Roll out the dough thinly and cut it into 2¾-inch / 7 cm squares. You should get about 30. Set aside on a tray sprinkled with cornmeal.

2. Heat the cooking oil in a large skillet over medium heat. Add the onion, garlic, and ¼ teaspoon salt, and cook, stirring often to prevent coloring, until softened, about 3 minutes. Add the Brussels sprouts, ¾ teaspoon salt, and the chestnuts (if using). Cook, stirring often, until the sprouts are browned in places but still vibrantly green, about 10 minutes. Sprinkle with black pepper. Taste and adjust the seasoning.

3. While the Brussels sprouts are cooking, in a bowl, whisk together the extra-virgin olive oil, lemon zest, and juice.

4. Bring salted water to a boil in a large saucepan. When the Brussels sprouts are just about done, add the pasta squares to the water one by one, to prevent sticking. Once they bob back to the surface, boil for 1 minute, until al dente. Drain and keep warm.

5. Arrange 6 warm pasta plates on your work surface. You will have to work fast so the food remains hot; you can ask someone to assist you. Onto each plate, scoop 5 mounds of the Brussels sprouts mixture, about 1 tablespoon each, and top each with a pasta square, picking it up with tongs or chopsticks. Drizzle with the lemon olive oil and top with a few shavings of cheese, if using. Serve immediately.

note You can make the pasta squares in advance and freeze in a single layer on a rimmed baking sheet sprinkled with cornmeal to prevent sticking. Once they are frozen solid, collect them in a freezer bag and return to the freezer for up to a month.

BRUSSELS SPROUTS

Too often boiled to a bitter mush, Brussels sprouts are a perfect delight when roasted but still a little crunchy in the middle (carve a deep "X" through the stem end to promote even cooking) or thinly sliced into ribbons and sautéed until browned in places but still leafy and alert, as in this recipe. When shopping for Brussels sprouts, pick small ones that look like tightly closed baby fists, with a healthy green color and no signs of yellowing. Use within a couple of days.

MUSHROOM AND CHIVE QUICHE

Quiche aux champignons à la ciboulette

While the quiche often has slight frou-frou connotations outside its birth country, it is nothing but the most homey and comforting of dishes in France, where it is among the first preparations beginner cooks learn to make. Indeed, once you've adopted a crust recipe you like and know the basic proportions for the custard filling, you can run away with the concept and garnish your quiches with whatever vegetables you want, or need, to use.

Mushrooms taste fantastic with anything cream- or egg-based, so I am very fond of them in a quiche. And because the dough can be prepared the day before and the mushrooms cooked some time in advance, too, this is a flexible dish to serve for a simple dinner with friends, possibly paired with the equally easygoing French Endive, Orange, and Walnut Salad (page 159).

1. Trim the mushrooms and cut into bite-size chunks; I prefer this to slices, as the morsels of mushrooms retain more of their meaty texture.

2. Heat a drizzle of oil in a large skillet over medium heat. Add the onion and ¼ teaspoon salt, and cook, stirring often, until softened, 4 minutes. Add the mushrooms and ½ teaspoon salt, and cook, stirring from time to time, until the mushrooms release their liquid, about 5 minutes. Increase the heat and simmer the mushrooms for a few more minutes, just enough for the excess liquid to evaporate. (However, if it looks like it will take more than 8 to 10 minutes to do this, it is better to drain the mushrooms than overcook them.)

RECIPE CONTINUES

SERVES 4 TO 6

2¼ pounds / 1 kg brown mushrooms or a mix of varieties

Olive oil for cooking

1 medium yellow onion (6 ounces / 170 g), finely sliced

Fine sea salt

Olive Oil Tart Dough (page 200)

All-purpose flour, for rolling

3 large organic eggs

⅓ cup / 80 ml heavy cream or unsweetened nondairy cream

½ cup / 120 ml milk (not skim) or unflavored, unsweetened nondairy milk

1 tablespoon Dijon mustard

2 teaspoons paprika

Freshly ground black pepper

½ cup / 20 g finely chopped fresh chives

This can be prepared a day ahead; let cool, cover, and refrigerate.

3. Remove the dough from the fridge 30 minutes before rolling out. Grease an 11- to 12-inch / 28 to 30 cm quiche pan.

4. Roll out the dough on a lightly floured surface to form a circle large enough to line your pan. Line the prepared pan with the dough, allowing a slight overhang of the dough around the rim of the pan. Prick the bottom all over with a fork, cover loosely with plastic wrap, and refrigerate for 30 minutes.

5. Preheat the oven to 325°F. / 160°C.

6. Remove the plastic from the quiche crust and bake for 20 minutes.

7. In the meantime, in a medium bowl, beat together the eggs, cream, milk, mustard, paprika, ½ teaspoon salt, and some black pepper.

8. Remove the crust from the oven and increase the oven temperature to 350°F. / 175°C. Spread the mushroom mixture evenly over the crust, sprinkle with the chives, and pour in the egg batter. Bake until set and lightly golden, about 45 minutes. Serve warm.

CAULIFLOWER GRATIN WITH TURMERIC AND HAZELNUTS

Gratin de choufleur au curcuma et noisettes

SERVES 4 TO 6

1 large head of cauliflower or 2 small ones, cut into florets (about 7 cups / 1 kg florets)

½ teaspoon fine sea salt

Freshly grated nutmeg

½ cup / 60 g hazelnuts, toasted (see page 68) and roughly chopped

½ cup / 40 g freshly grated Comté or Gruyère cheese (optional)

½ teaspoon turmeric

Béchamel Sauce (page 213)

2 tablespoons plain dried bread crumbs

I know many people who dislike cauliflower. Perhaps I am biased since I grew up eating my mother's killer *gratin de choufleur,* but I don't see what's not to like about a vegetable that's mild-flavored without being bland, as comforting as mashed potatoes when cooked to tenderness, and so good-looking it is described as a flower in numerous languages.

This gratin is particularly successful for recruiting new converts: it is a riff on my mother's, to which I've added turmeric for flavor and color, and a sprinkle of hazelnuts for crunch. The pairing is serendipitously inspired by a loaf of turmeric and hazelnut bread by Paris baker Eric Kayser, which I once ate with a cauliflower soup I'd just made.

The gratin can be prepared ahead in part and it is a good occasion to try your hand at béchamel sauce if you've never made it before. The gratin can be made vegan, if you prefer, by omitting the cheese (or replacing it with ¼ cup nutritional yeast) and using the vegan variation of the béchamel.

1. Set up a steamer. Steam the cauliflower florets, tightly covered, until tender, 10 to 15 minutes. They may be cooked up to a day in advance; once cool, refrigerate in an airtight container.

2. Arrange the cauliflower in a shallow 2-quart / 2-liter baking dish. Season with the salt and a touch of nutmeg and top with the hazelnuts and half of the grated cheese (if using).

RECIPE CONTINUES

3. Preheat the oven to 350°F. / 175°C.

4. Whisk the turmeric into the béchamel sauce until well blended and pour evenly over the cauliflower. Sprinkle with the remaining cheese (if using) and the bread crumbs.

5. Bake until golden, 20 to 30 minutes, switching to the broiler setting for the final few minutes for optimal browning. Let stand for 5 minutes before serving.

CAULIFLOWER

A good head of cauliflower should be creamy white, with no grayish hints, and the florets should be firm and tightly bunched up. Pay attention to the outer leaves, too; they are a good indication of freshness. To use, pull off the outer leaves (save for stock, see page 198) and then use a sharp knife to separate the white part into evenly sized florets. The stem of the cauliflower can be saved for soup.

1½ cups / 300 g
spelt berries

2 tablespoons
olive oil for cooking

2 small red onions
(4¼ ounces / 120 g
each), thinly sliced

Fine sea salt

1 medium leek
(11 ounces / 300 g),
trimmed, carefully
washed and thinly
sliced

2 medium / 250 g
carrots, peeled
and diced

8 ounces / 225 g
Jerusalem
artichokes, peeled
and diced

¾ teaspoon finely
chopped dried
rosemary

½ cup / 120 ml dry
white wine

3 cups / 720 ml
Vegetable Stock
(page 198), heated to
a simmer

1 cup / 20 g chopped
fresh flat-leaf parsley
leaves

Freshly ground
black pepper

SPELT AND VEGETABLE PILAF
Pilaf d'épeautre aux petits légumes

Pilaf is a classic cooking method for rice in which the grain is first sautéed with onions and a bit of fat (often butter), covered with water or stock, and left to cook undisturbed in a covered pot, usually in the oven. This produces a notably tender and flavorful rice, and I have found that it can be applied just as successfully to other grains, such as spelt. What's convenient about the method is that it needs minimal attention while the grain cooks, so you can tend to your other duties.

Rather than cook the grain solo, I add vegetables so they'll contribute their flavor to the dish and make it a one-pot meal. I like this version with leeks, carrots, and Jerusalem artichokes, but any mix of seasonal vegetables will work, as long as they're cut into small enough pieces that they'll cook at the same rate as the grain. Sometimes I top it with a fried egg. Leftovers may be eaten cold over the next day or two, blended into a salad of chopped mixed greens.

1. If you have the forethought, put the spelt in a bowl a few hours beforehand, cover with cold water, and let stand on the counter. Otherwise, simply rinse the spelt before starting.

2. Preheat the oven to 400°F. / 200°C.

3. Heat the olive oil in a Dutch oven over medium heat. Add the onions and ½ teaspoon salt, stir, and cook until softened, about 5 minutes.

4. Drain the spelt well, add to the pot along with another ½ teaspoon salt, and cook, stirring often, for 5 minutes. Add the leek, carrots, Jerusalem artichokes, rosemary, and ½ teaspoon salt. Pour in the wine, bring

to a low simmer, and cook until the wine is reduced to a glaze, about 5 minutes.

5. Stir in the stock, cover, and bake until the spelt is cooked through and the liquids are absorbed, 40 to 50 minutes. Check halfway through that there is some liquid left in the pot; add a little hot water if it's running low.

6. Let stand on the counter, covered, for 10 minutes. Stir in the parsley, sprinkle with black pepper, and serve.

pantry gem

SPELT, EMMER WHEAT, AND EINKORN WHEAT

Spelt, emmer wheat (sometimes sold as farro), and einkorn wheat are ancient cousins of wheat, domesticated and first cultivated millennia ago. Higher-yield crops have long displaced these nutritious grains, but they are now regaining popularity in the Western world—in whole grain, flour, or rolled grain form—as conscious eaters try to add variety to their diet and not rely so heavily on common wheat, which is often highly processed.

Einkorn wheat is the favored variety in France: *petit épeautre de Haute Provence* is believed to have been grown in the southeast of France unchanged, i.e., without crossbreeding, for 9,000 years, and has PGI (protected geographical indication) status.

**1 cup / 230 g French
green lentils**

**1 small yellow onion
(4¼ ounces / 120 g),
finely diced**

**2 cups / 480 ml
Vegetable Stock
(page 198)**

**1 teaspoon fine
sea salt**

**¼ cup / 35 g
all-purpose flour**

1 large organic egg

**¼ cup / 40 g plain
dried bread crumbs**

**½ cup / 20 g very
finely chopped fresh
flat-leaf parsley
leaves**

**1 garlic clove,
finely chopped**

**1 teaspoon ground
coriander**

**Herbed Tahini Sauce
(page 214)**

LENTIL CROQUETTES
Croquettes de lentilles

Few foods are as nutritious and satisfying as lentils, which also
happen to be quite versatile, making them easy to incorporate
into your meals. An option that's often overlooked is the
croquette, which could be described as the legume's answer to
meatballs: cooked lentils are shaped into balls, battered, and
baked in the oven until they form a crisp outer crust, while the
inside remains tender.

I serve these croquettes warm, over a zesty salad of grated
carrots, with an herbed tahini sauce drizzled on top, as you
might a plate of falafel. This recipe can also give new life to
leftover cooked lentils: you'll need 2¼ cups / 450 g cooked lentils
for the full recipe, but it can be scaled up or down to match the
amount of lentils you have on hand.

1. A day before serving, cook the lentils: In a medium
   saucepan, combine the lentils, onion, and stock.
   Cover and bring to a simmer over medium heat. Cook
   until the lentils are fairly soft so they can be shaped
   into balls, 20 to 30 minutes depending on the lentils.
   Drain well, and stir in the salt. Cool completely and
   refrigerate overnight.

2. Preheat the oven to 400°F. / 200°C. and line a baking
   sheet with parchment paper or a silicone baking mat.

3. Set up 3 wide shallow bowls. Put the flour in one.
   Lightly beat the egg in the second. Put the bread
   crumbs in the third. Arrange the bowls and the
   prepared baking sheet on the counter in an assembly
   line.

4. Add the parsley, garlic, and coriander to the cooked lentils and stir well to combine. With moist hands, scoop out a small handful of this mixture, about the size of a golf ball. Squeeze to remove excess moisture and shape into a ball between the palms of your hands. If you find the lentils resist shaping, mash them slightly with a potato masher—don't turn them to a complete mush, just enough for them to hold together.

5. Dip into the flour to coat lightly, then into the egg, and then the bread crumbs. Put the breaded croquette on the prepared baking sheet.

6. Rinse your hands (keep a bowl of water on the counter for that purpose) and repeat with the rest of the lentils; you should get a dozen croquettes.

7. Bake until golden and crusty, about 30 minutes.

BREAD CRUMBS

There are many ways to upcycle staling leftover bread, including making Garlic Rosemary Croutons (page 111) or Tomato and Tarragon Bread Soup (page 72), but the easiest is to turn them into bread crumbs. Dice the leftover bread and leave it out on the counter to dry completely. (In humid weather, dry the bread in a low oven without allowing it to brown.) Grind in the bowl of a sturdy food processor, or in batches in a spice grinder, until reduced to coarse crumbs. Transfer to a jar and use within a few months. You could season the bread crumbs with salt, spices, or dried herbs, but they'll be more versatile if you leave them unseasoned.

SAVORY PUMPKIN AND CORNMEAL QUICK BREAD

Cake au potiron et semoule de maïs

This recipe is inspired by *méture,* a rustic bread from the Landes region in the Southwest of France. This all-but-forgotten loaf, made with corn flour, was baked on farms where a small portion of the corn harvest was set aside for the household.

I once read about a *méture au potiron,* made with pumpkin, and although I was unable to find a recipe for it, the idea lodged itself in my head and emerged one day in the form of this moist quick bread, flavored with herbs and walnuts.

In France, we simply call such loaves *cakes*—pronounced with a French accent—and serve them by the slice at buffets and picnics or in bite-size cubes to accompany a predinner drink. Pack some for lunch to pair with a salad or a soup.

1. Peel and seed the pumpkin and then cut it into ½-inch / 1 cm chunks. Set up a steamer. Steam the pumpkin, tightly covered, until soft, 8 to 12 minutes depending on the pumpkin. Put through a ricer or food mill.

2. Transfer to a fine-mesh sieve and set over a bowl to cool and drain for 1 hour, stirring gently from time to time to encourage the juices to drain; pumpkins tend to release a fair amount of liquid, but if you've used another type of squash, there may not be much to drain at all. This should yield about 2 cups / 340 g drained pumpkin flesh.

RECIPE CONTINUES

MAKES ONE
9 x 5-INCH /
23 x 12 CM LOAF

1¾-pound / 800 g wedge of baking pumpkin or winter squash

2 tablespoons olive oil for cooking, plus more for the pan

¾ cup / 120 g fine-grind stone-ground cornmeal, plus more for sprinkling

¾ cup / 100 g all-purpose flour, sifted

2 teaspoons baking powder

1½ teaspoons fine sea salt

¼ teaspoon freshly ground black pepper

1 cup (100 g) walnut halves, toasted (see page 68) and roughly chopped

3 large organic eggs

1 cup / 20 g chopped fresh chervil or flat-leaf parsley leaves

3. Preheat the oven to 350°F. / 175°C. Grease a 9 × 5-inch / 23 × 12 cm loaf pan with oil, line the bottom with parchment paper, and sprinkle the sides with cornmeal until entirely coated.

4. In a medium bowl, combine the cornmeal, flour, baking powder, salt, pepper, and walnuts.

5. In a large bowl, beat together the cooked pumpkin, eggs, 2 tablespoons oil, and the chervil. Fold in the flour mixture with a spatula just until no trace of flour remains; avoid overmixing, or the texture of the loaf will be heavier.

6. Pour into the prepared pan and level out the surface. Bake until the top is crusty and golden and a knife inserted in the middle comes out clean, 40 to 45 minutes.

7. Transfer to a rack. Let cool for 20 minutes before turning out, and serve slightly warm or at room temperature.

note Season the drained pumpkin juices with celery salt, black pepper, and hot sauce for a simplified Virgin Mary.

PERSONALIZED DINNER ROLLS
Petits pains personnalisés

MAKES 8
DINNER ROLLS

For the bread dough

3⅔ cups / 470 g
bread flour, plus
more for dusting

2 teaspoons / 10 g
fine sea salt

¼ teaspoon active
dry yeast

When I was growing up, our neighborhood bakery displayed bread rolls with first names written on them in edible ink. It seemed to me the height of sophistication. I must have been ten the day I decided to secretly place an order for each member of my family and sneak out before Sunday lunch to get them. I put them on the table, and beamed as my parents and sister discovered my surprise.

I forgot all about these until fifteen years later, when I took a bread-baking class and the instructor whipped out a small piping cone to write on the baguettes we had just shaped. I made sure I got his recipe for edible writing paste and have used it since to personalize my own dinner rolls. You can use them in lieu of place cards when you have guests or come up with a design to match the theme of an event you may be hosting.

This writing paste works for any bread dough, including these no-knead dinner rolls, adapted from a method that baker Jim Lahey and writer Mark Bittman popularized some years ago. It produces flavorful mini loaves with a crisp crust and a moist crumb.

1. In a large bowl, combine the flour, salt, and yeast. Pour in 1½ cups / 360 ml room-temperature water and mix with a wooden spoon or dough whisk until the dough comes together in a shaggy ball. Cover the bowl with plastic wrap and let stand at room temperature (around 70°F / 20°C) until roughly doubled in size and the surface is covered with little bubbles, 12 to 18 hours.

RECIPE CONTINUES

For the writing paste

1 large organic egg white

2 tablespoons all-purpose flour

1 tablespoon unsweetened Dutch-process cocoa powder

2. In a small bowl, whisk together the egg white, flour, and cocoa powder until completely smooth. The writing paste should be the consistency of chocolate pudding: not too thin, or it will dribble, and not too thick, or you'll have difficulties piping it.

3. Make a small paper cone using a triangular piece of parchment paper. (This is called a cornet, and you can find online videos demonstrating the folding technique.) Spoon in the writing paste, fold the opening shut two or three times, and refrigerate for up to a day.

4. Have ready two baking sheets lined with parchment paper or silicone baking mats.

5. When the dough is ready, turn it out on a well-floured surface. Divide it into 8 equal pieces, and shape each of them into a tightly formed dinner roll, keeping your hands floured to prevent sticking. Place on the prepared baking sheets.

6. Snip off the very tip of the cornet—you want a very small opening so the paste comes out thinly to form clean letters—and pipe the writing paste onto the rolls as desired. Friends and children can be enlisted to help. (Scrape any leftover writing paste into a small container and freeze for future use.)

7. Place an ovenproof cast-iron pan on the floor of the oven and preheat the oven to the highest temperature setting, at least 475°F. / 250°C., for 30 minutes. Have ready ½ cup / 120 ml boiling water in a pouring jug.

8. Using a razor blade or a very sharp knife, cut a lengthwise slit in each of the rolls just above your text; this will promote the rise of the rolls and prevent their crust from tearing randomly through your lettering.

9. Place the two baking sheets in the oven quickly and, wearing long sleeves and an oven mitt, pour the boiling water into the cast-iron pan before closing the oven door; the steam will help form a crisp crust.

10. Reduce the oven temperature to 450°F. / 230°C. Bake the rolls for 15 minutes. Switch the position of the two baking sheets, reduce the oven temperature to 350°F. / 175°C., and bake until golden brown, 15 to 25 minutes. Transfer to a rack to cool before serving.

11. You can make these in advance, cool completely, and freeze. Thaw overnight on the counter and return to a 350°F. / 175°C. oven for 5 minutes to refresh.

SERVES 6

½ cup / 120 ml strong coffee, unsweetened

Seeds from 6 green cardamom pods, finely ground, or ¾ teaspoon ground green cardamom

2 to 3 level tablespoons mild honey, to taste

2 cups / 480 ml plain all-natural Greek yogurt

6½ ounces / 185 g ladyfingers (about 30)

¾ cup / 85 g unsalted pistachios, halved

2 ounces / 55 g good-quality bittersweet chocolate (about 65% cacao), chilled

LEBANESE COFFEE DESSERT JARS
Verrines "café libanais"

Every few Saturdays, Maxence and I have lunch at a tiny Lebanese restaurant in our neighborhood. It's little more than a take-out counter, but there are a couple of tables at which to sit and share a plate of hummus while we wait for our falafel sandwiches.

And when we're done, the owner asks if we would care for a *café libanais*, a thickly steeped coffee flavored with cardamom. It is much too strong for me, but I do revel in the paired scents of coffee and cardamom wafting up from the small tin pot. Occasionally, it is brought to our table with a complimentary plate of baklava, two-bite crunchy pastries loaded with pistachios and honey, and it is the memory of those flavors coming together in beautiful harmony—coffee, cardamom, pistachio, honey—that inspired this simple dessert.

I dip ladyfingers in cardamom-flavored coffee and top them with honeyed yogurt, pistachios, and grated chocolate. It is a delicious and remarkably low-effort dessert that can be prepared a few hours in advance, and looks equally lovely served in matching or mismatched containers.

1. Have ready 6 transparent jars or glasses, about ½ cup / 120 ml in capacity.

2. In a small saucepan combine the coffee and cardamom. Bring just under a simmer over low heat, remove from the heat, and set aside to cool.

3. Stir 2 tablespoons honey into the yogurt. Add more to taste; it should be pleasantly sweet, but not overly so.

RECIPE CONTINUES

4. Cut the ladyfingers into bite-size pieces. Quickly dip half of these pieces in the cardamom coffee and divide among the glasses, arranging them more or less in a single layer at the bottom. (If your ladyfingers fall apart when dipped, place them dry in the glass and brush with the coffee instead of dipping.)

5. Spoon the sweetened yogurt over the ladyfingers, about 2½ tablespoons per glass. Sprinkle with half of the pistachios, dividing them equally among the glasses, and grate chocolate on top using a zester or vegetable peeler.

6. Repeat the layers—coffee-dipped ladyfingers, yogurt, and pistachios, but *not* the grated chocolate—using up the remaining ingredients.

7. Cover and refrigerate for 2 hours or overnight, removing from the fridge 30 minutes before serving. Grate the remaining chocolate then (if you do it earlier, it will absorb moisture in the fridge and won't look as pretty).

APPLE SUGAR TART

Tarte au sucre aux pommes

My grandmother was born and raised in a small town in the North of France right on the Belgian border, in a region that has a strong identity with its own patois, folk tales, and culinary repertoire. She's the one who tipped me off to the sugar tart, known in the North as *l'tart à chuc*: a round of light, brioche-like dough made with beer or milk, topped with a mix of sugar and crème fraîche, and baked to a golden amber.

It is irresistible as is, but I have taken the liberty of removing the cream topping and adding in its stead thinly sliced apples, fanned out across the top of the tart; they add a welcome layer of fruity and lightly tart notes and nothing's stopping you from dolloping crème fraîche on the side when you serve it.

The dough base itself is not very sweet at all; most of the sugar is in fact sprinkled on the tart, where it is in a prime position to caramelize in the oven. The ideal sugar to use here would be the locally produced *vergeoise brune,* a brown beet sugar with notes of butterscotch; short of that, you can use any flavorful soft, light brown sugar.

SERVES 8

⅔ cup / 160 ml amber beer or milk

½ teaspoon active dry yeast

2 cups / 260 g all-purpose flour

¼ teaspoon fine sea salt

⅔ cup packed / 115 g soft, light brown sugar

1 large organic egg

7 tablespoons / 100 g high-quality unsalted butter, softened, plus more for the pan

1 pound / 450 g baking apples (Jonagold, Gala, and Braeburn are good choices, but do try lesser-known, local varieties)

Crème fraîche, sour cream, or vanilla ice cream, for serving

1. In a small saucepan, heat the beer to lukewarm (when you dip your finger in, you shouldn't feel any temperature difference). Add the yeast, and let rest for 10 minutes. After that time, active yeast will form a slightly foamy layer at the surface; if it doesn't, get a fresh package and try again.

2. In the bowl of a stand mixer fitted with the dough hook, combine the flour, salt, and 2 tablespoons of the brown sugar. Add the yeast mixture, the egg, and butter and knead at low speed for 10 minutes.

RECIPE CONTINUES

(Alternatively, you can work by hand in a large bowl, using a wooden spoon or dough whisk; the dough is too soft to knead by hand.)

3. Cover with plastic wrap and let rest at room temperature for 1½ hours, or overnight in the refrigerator (after refrigeration, let rest at room temperature for 30 minutes before using).

4. Preheat the oven to 400°F. / 200°C. and grease an 11- to 12-inch / 28 to 30 cm tart pan with a pat of butter.

5. Scrape the dough into the pan and spread it with a spatula to cover the surface of the pan evenly. Sprinkle with two-thirds of the remaining sugar; it will seem like a lot of sugar, but remember there is hardly any in the dough itself.

6. Peel and core the apples and then slice them horizontally into very thin rounds, using a mandoline slicer or very sharp knife. Arrange on the dough in a circular, tightly overlapping pattern, starting from the outside and leaving a ¾-inch / 2 cm margin of uncovered dough all around. Sprinkle with the remaining sugar.

7. Bake for 20 minutes. Cover loosely with foil and then bake until golden brown and caramelized, 15 to 25 minutes more.

8. Serve slightly warm or at room temperature, with crème fraîche.

For the syrup

½ cup / 100 g unrefined blond cane sugar (also sold as evaporated cane juice)

2 tablespoons freshly squeezed lemon juice

Zest of ½ organic orange (grated, or thinly peeled with a vegetable peeler)

½ star anise

½ cinnamon stick

2 whole cloves

Seeds from 4 green cardamom pods, or ½ teaspoon ground green cardamom

For the salad

2 organic oranges

4 kiwifruit

3 pears

2 small bananas

1 teaspoon orange flower water, or more to taste (optional)

FRUIT SALAD WITH SPICED SYRUP

Salade de fruits au sirop d'épices

A good fruit salad, prepared carefully and well seasoned, can be a sublime thing. The first order of business is to select the fruit: seek variety in texture (crisp, crunchy, soft) and flavor (sweet, tart, floral) and seasonal fruit that is ripe, so it tastes its best, but not so ripe it will turn to mush in the salad bowl. Good winter fruits to use include pears, apples, kiwis, persimmons, and citrus as well as tropical fruits (bananas, mangoes, passion fruit), though these last in moderation due to their faraway provenance; choose ones preferably from a fair-trade source. You are looking for roughly 3⅓ pounds / 1.5 kg total fruit.

But the real magic lies in the spiced syrup stirred into the fruit; it highlights their sweetness without overstating it and adds a dimension of flavor that elevates the fruit salad from a basic blend of cut-up fruit to something that stops guests in their tracks and makes them go for seconds.

I serve fruit salads with a cookie partner, such as Lemon Corn Cookies (page 56) or Breton Shortbread Cookies (page 45). It's also an excellent complement to a sliver of rich chocolate cake.

1. Prepare the syrup up to a day ahead. In a small saucepan, combine the sugar, lemon juice, orange zest, star anise, cinnamon stick, cloves, cardamom, and ¾ cup / 180 ml cold water. Bring to a simmer over medium heat and cook for 10 minutes. Let cool completely.

2. Prepare the salad. Peel and core the fruit as needed and cut into bite-size pieces. Place in a medium salad

bowl and pour in the syrup through a fine-mesh sieve (discard the spices). Add the orange flower water (if using) and stir gently to coat.

3. Cover and refrigerate for 1 to 2 hours, removing from the fridge 30 minutes before serving. Leftovers are delicious the next day, though the fruit will look a little less perky then.

CHOCOLATE BERAWECKA
Berawecka au chocolat

Berawecka is an Alsatian specialty that pops up in local pastry shops and market stalls during Advent, the weeks leading up to Christmas. It is a small loaf chock-full of dried fruits, candied citrus, and nuts, bound by just enough bread dough to hold it all together. Not too sweet—there is no sugar added beyond that of the fruit—but crunchy, moist, and flavorful, it is the perfect winter treat, the kind that would feel nutritious and restorative in the middle of a snowshoe hike or just a long and gray afternoon spent at your desk. I add chocolate to my own take on the traditional recipe in the form of cocoa powder and chopped chocolate. Unsurprisingly, I like it even better that way.

Berawecka is meant to be baked some time in advance, wrapped tightly, and left to "ripen" for a few weeks before eating in thin slices, with a cup of tea or mulled wine. It is delicious the day it is baked, but during this resting period, the flavors will bloom and the texture will even out for easier slicing. This also makes it an ideal holiday food gift to bake and ship out before things get too hectic.

1. Sort through your dried fruits and separate the moist and sticky ones (prunes, figs, dates) from the leathery ones (pears, apples, mangoes). Place the second group in a heatproof bowl and pour in hot water just to cover. Set aside for 10 minutes to soften and then drain, keeping the soaking water.

2. Chop all the dried fruits into small dice; some may be easier to chop using kitchen shears as opposed to a knife. Combine in a medium bowl with the candied citrus and kirsch. Set aside to soak.

RECIPE CONTINUES

MAKES FOUR
12-OUNCE / 350 G
LOAVES

14 ounces / 340 g mixed **dried fruits** (pears, apples, dates, figs, prunes, cranberries, cherries, mangoes, etc.)

5 ounces / 140 g **candied citrus**, finely diced

¼ cup / 60 ml kirsch, **Grand Marnier**, or other **fruit brandy** or **liqueur**, or **black tea**

7 ounces / 200 g mixed **nuts** (almonds, walnuts, hazelnuts, etc.), including **12 whole almonds**

½ teaspoon active **dry yeast**

2½ cups / 325 g **all-purpose flour**

1 teaspoon **fine sea salt**

1 teaspoon warm **spice mix**, such as pumpkin pie or gingerbread spices (clove, ginger, cinnamon, and nutmeg)

¼ cup / 30 g unsweetened Dutch-process **cocoa powder**

7 ounces / 200 g good-quality bittersweet **chocolate** (about 65% cacao), chopped to chocolate chip–size bits

3. Set the 12 almonds aside in a small bowl with just enough water to cover (this prevents them from burning in the oven). Chop the rest of the nuts roughly.

4. Measure the soaking water saved from the dried fruits and add or remove water as needed to get ⅓ cup / 80 ml. In a small saucepan, heat the soaking water to lukewarm (when you dip your finger in, you shouldn't feel any temperature difference). Add the yeast, and let rest for 10 minutes. After that time, active yeast will form a slightly foamy layer at the surface; if it doesn't, get a fresh package and try again.

5. In a large bowl, combine 2 cups/260 g of the flour with the salt. Add the yeast and water and stir with a fork or a dough whisk until the dough comes together; add a little more water as needed to get a shaggy but not too tacky dough. Cover and let rest until doubled in volume, 1½ hours.

6. Preheat the oven to 350°F. / 175°C. and line a baking sheet with parchment paper or a silicone baking mat.

7. Add the spices and cocoa powder to the fruits and stir to combine. Add the fruit mixture, along with the chopped nuts, chocolate, and remaining flour, to the bread dough. Stir vigorously until completely combined, using a dough whisk or your hands as preferred and adding a little water if necessary. You'll get a rather messy, sticky dough.

8. Divide the dough into 4 equal pieces and transfer to the prepared sheet with a spatula, coaxing each into the shape of a football.

9. Gently press 3 soaked almonds along the spine of each loaf. Bake for 20 minutes. Cover loosely with foil and bake until the loaves are slightly puffy and completely set, 30 to 40 minutes more.

10. Transfer to a rack to cool completely.

DRIED FRUITS

Despite their name, dried fruits should not be dry, leathery little pucks. They should be wrinkled, yes, but they should feel plump and fleshy when you squeeze them gently. Buy them from a grower who produces the fresh fruit and dries the excess crop, if you can, or from the bulk section of a natural foods store. If you buy them in a package, make sure they contain no additives or preservatives. Buy in small amounts and use within a few months of purchase. If they seem too dry, soak in hot water or tea for a few hours to plump them back up.

ESSENTIALS

Les essentiels

MAKES 2 QUARTS /
2 LITERS

**1 tablespoon olive oil
for cooking**

**1 medium yellow
onion (6 ounces /
170 g), roughly
chopped (not peeled)**

**2 medium / 250 g
carrots, sliced
(not peeled)**

**2 stalks / 250 g
celery, sliced**

**2 garlic cloves,
smashed with the
flat of a knife blade**

**2 teaspoons
fine sea salt**

**6 black peppercorns,
crushed with the flat
of a knife blade**

**1 prune or 1 table-
spoon tomato paste**

2 whole cloves

**1 bay leaf, fresh
or dried**

**A few sprigs of
thyme, fresh or dried**

**1 sprig of rosemary,
fresh or dried**

**A splash of dry
white wine
(optional)**

VEGETABLE STOCK
Bouillon de légumes

In my early years as a cook, I resisted the notion of homemade
stock with all my might. But so many sources recommended it
that I felt I should at least *try,* and I had to admit it did take my
dishes to a whole new level.

It is now my duty to pass on that life lesson; homemade
vegetable stock is plenty worth your time. And the effort is, in
truth, minimal. Feel free to play with this formula, depending
on what you have in the fridge and in the stock box you should
keep in your freezer.

1. Heat the oil in a stockpot over medium heat. Add the
   onion, carrots, celery, garlic, and salt, and cook for
   about 5 minutes, stirring often, until lightly colored.
   Add the rest of the ingredients and 2 quarts / 2 liters
   cold water.

2. Cover, bring to a simmer, and cook for 30 minutes. Set
   a fine-mesh sieve over a large bowl and use a ladle to
   transfer the vegetables and stock into the sieve. Drain
   completely without pressing. Use the stock right away
   or let cool completely before refrigerating or freezing
   in airtight containers.

KEEPING A STOCK BOX

Stock can also be flavored with mushrooms and mushroom
trimmings, leek greens, fennel and fennel trimmings, onion
peels, pea pods, and herb stems, all of which you can
collect in a dedicated "stock box" in the freezer whenever
you use these vegetables.

YOGURT TART DOUGH
Pâte à tarte au yaourt

Using a mix of yogurt and butter produces a particularly crisp and flaky crust that makes vegetable tarts feel as rewarding as dessert. It can be made with just all-purpose flour, but sometimes I like to use some buckwheat flour for a malty variation.

1. In a medium bowl, whisk the flour to remove any lumps. Form a well in the center and spoon in the yogurt. Add the butter and salt and use a pastry blender, a sturdy fork, or the tips of your fingers to rub the yogurt and butter into the flour. (Alternatively, mix the dough in short pulses in a food processor.)

2. When most of the flour is incorporated and you can no longer see pieces of butter in the dough, turn out onto a clean work surface and knead the dough lightly until it comes together into a ball. Add a little flour or a few drops of water to reach a workable consistency. Flatten it into a thick disk or square, to match the shape of the tart you plan to make. Wrap in plastic and refrigerate for 30 minutes or overnight (return to just below room temperature before using).

Buckwheat Variation Use 1 cup / 130 g all-purpose flour plus ½ cup / 65 g buckwheat flour.

MAKES ENOUGH FOR ONE 11-INCH / 28 CM TART

1½ cups / 195 g all-purpose flour

½ cup plus 1 tablespoon / 130 g plain all-natural yogurt (not nonfat) or silken tofu

5 tablespoons / 65 g cold high-quality unsalted butter, diced, or ⅓ cup / 80 ml olive oil

½ teaspoon fine sea salt

¼ cup / 60 ml olive
oil for cooking, plus
more for the pan

2 cups / 260 g
all-purpose flour,
plus more for dusting

1 teaspoon fine
sea salt

1 tablespoon sesame
seeds, toasted
(optional; see
page 68)

1 tablespoon poppy
seeds (optional)

1 large organic egg

1 large organic
egg white (optional)

OLIVE OIL TART DOUGH
Pâte à tarte à l'huile d'olive

As much as I love a good short-crust pastry, in recent years I
have adopted another way of making savory tart crusts, using
olive oil instead of butter.

This dough is even easier to work with than one made
with butter; it comes together by hand in minutes, calls for
ingredients I always have available, and lets itself be rolled out
amenably, thanks to its flexible yet cohesive consistency. It
bakes into a lightly crunchy, flavorsome crust that is much less
susceptible to sogginess if your filling is on the wet side. It also
keeps well—improves, even—from the first day to the next.

I sometimes mix in sesame and poppy seeds for looks and
crunch, but dried herbs work well, too, or you can omit these
adornments altogether.

1. Have ready an 11- to 12-inch / 28 to 30 cm tart pan
   and oil it lightly.

2. In a medium bowl, combine the flour, salt, and seeds
   (if using). Add the oil, egg, and ¼ cup / 60 ml cold
   water and mix them in with a fork or dough whisk
   until absorbed. Turn the dough out onto a lightly
   floured work surface and knead lightly until it comes
   together into a ball. Add a little more water or flour as
   necessary.

3. Dust the ball of dough and a rolling pin with flour
   and roll the dough out into a round large enough to
   fit the tart pan. Give the dough a quarter turn every
   time you roll the pin and back, and add a little more
   flour under and on top of the dough when it seems on
   the verge of becoming sticky. The trick is to roll it out

in quick, assertive gestures to avoid overworking the dough.

4. Transfer the dough to the prepared pan and line it neatly. Trim the excess dough (see Note) and place the pan in the fridge for 30 minutes or up to a day.

5. For use with juicy fillings, brush the crust with egg white, prick with a fork, and bake on its own for 30 minutes in a preheated 325°F. / 160°C. oven before filling. For dryer fillings, you can top the uncooked dough with no prior baking.

note Arrange the trimmings on a greased baking sheet, brush with oil, sprinkle with salt, and bake for 10 minutes at 400°F. / 200°C. for a cook's snack.

SERVES 4 AS
A MAIN DISH

**1¼ cups / 160 g
all-purpose flour,
plus more as needed**

**⅔ cup / 80 g
buckwheat flour**

**½ teaspoon
fine sea salt**

**3 large organic eggs
(about 5¾ ounces /
160 g weighed
without the shell)**

BUCKWHEAT PASTA DOUGH
Pâte à pâtes au sarrasin

As kids, when my sister and I would announce we were bored, my mother would make us a batch of salt dough for modeling. We would sit at the small fold-out table in the kitchen and squeeze and roll and pinch to our hearts' content.

The memory of these childhood episodes was awakened when I first tried my hand at homemade pasta; pasta dough is a most pleasant dough to handle, silky smooth and wonderfully cooperative, and working with it truly feels like child's play.

I've adopted the formula Michael Ruhlman shares in his seminal book about ratios; two parts egg to three parts flour (by weight) creates the perfect consistency and allows you to try different flours, provided they have enough gluten for the dough to remain pliable. I like to use two-thirds all-purpose flour and one-third buckwheat flour, for a nice flavor complexity.

1. In a medium bowl, combine the flours and salt. Make a well in the center and break the eggs into it. Using a fork or dough whisk, stir in the eggs.

2. When the dough comes together, turn it out onto a lightly floured work surface and knead until soft and smooth, about 8 minutes. (Alternatively, this can be done in the bowl of a stand mixer fitted with the paddle attachment.) The dough should not be tacky; add a little more flour if necessary. Cover with a kitchen towel and let rest for 30 minutes. (You can also prepare it a day in advance, wrap it in plastic, and refrigerate.)

3. Have ready four wooden clothes hangers, horizontal bar wiped clean, dried, and lightly dusted with flour.

4. Divide the dough into 4 equal pieces. Take one piece of dough (keep the others covered) and flatten into an oval disk. Dust lightly with flour.

5. Set the roller of a pasta machine on the widest setting, slip in the disk of dough, and run it through. Fold in half so the two short sides meet and slip it into the roller fold-side first, and run it through again. Repeat until the dough feels supple—this step essentially kneads the dough again—and is a fairly even rectangular shape. If it gets sticky at any point, dust with a little flour.

6. Switch the pasta roller to the next narrower setting and run the dough through to thin it out, just once this time. Repeat with the subsequent settings until you reach the thickness of your choice. (If the dough tears at any point, the kneading step may have been too short; fold the dough back into a small rectangle, and start again from the widest setting.)

7. Dust the sheet of dough lightly with flour, slip onto the bar of one of the prepared hangers, and hang to dry at least 15 minutes, while you work on the remaining pieces of dough.

8. The pasta dough is now ready to be cut, using the blades of the pasta roller to make fettuccine or spaghetti, or by hand to make ravioli and all sorts of hand-cut pasta shapes. You can also use the sheets of dough to make lasagna or cannelloni. Let the cut pasta dry for another 15 minutes before cooking or freezing.

9. To cook fresh pasta, plunge it into a large pot of boiling salted water; if your pot is too small, the pasta may clump up. Stir gently during the first moments of

RECIPE CONTINUES

cooking so the pieces don't stick to the bottom of the pan, then cook for a minute after the pasta rises to the surface. Taste for doneness, drain, and serve. Cook frozen pasta in the same manner, without thawing.

note If buckwheat flour is unavailable, use a scant 2 cups / 240 g all-purpose flour total instead.

---

pantry gem

BUCKWHEAT FLOUR

Buckwheat flour is traditionally used to make savory crêpes in Brittany, but also blini in Russia and soba noodles in Japan. Its flavor is rather assertive in a nutty kind of way, so it is best used in partnership with a milder flour.

Buckwheat pairs well with carrots, mushrooms, asparagus, berries, and plums, and I love to slip the flour into breads, pasta, cookies, and pancakes. In this book, look for it in Asparagus Buckwheat Tart (page 40) and Buckwheat and Brussels Sprouts Open Ravioli (page 166).

SPELT TART DOUGH
Pâte à tarte à l'épeautre

MAKES ENOUGH
FOR ONE
DOUBLE-CRUST
11-INCH / 28 CM
PIE

A yeast-raised crust gives vegetable tarts a slightly rustic feel that I find very appealing. Such crusts hold up better to the juices of moist fillings, too, and make tarts easy to transport and eat out of hand for a picnic. This version calls for spelt flour, which I like to use in place of wheat flour for a change of pace.

2 cups plus
2 tablespoons /
280 g spelt flour or
all-purpose flour

½ teaspoon active
dry yeast

1 teaspoon
fine sea salt

2 tablespoons olive
oil for cooking

1. In a medium bowl, combine the flour with ½ cup / 120 ml cold water using a dough whisk or fork. Let rest for 30 minutes to allow the flour to absorb the water.

2. In a small bowl, dissolve the yeast in 2 tablespoons lukewarm water (when you dip your finger in, you shouldn't feel any temperature difference) and let rest for 10 minutes. After that time, active yeast will form a slightly foamy layer at the surface; if it doesn't, get a fresh package and try again. Add to the dough along with the salt and olive oil, and stir to combine.

3. Turn out onto a lightly floured work surface and knead until the dough is smooth and pulls away from the counter, about 5 minutes. The dough will remain fairly tacky; adjust the consistency with a little more water or flour as needed.

4. Return to the bowl, cover with plastic wrap, and let rest at room temperature until puffy, 2 hours. The dough can be made up to a day in advance: refrigerate just after kneading and remove from the fridge 2 hours before using.

MAKES ABOUT
½ CUP / 120 ML
DRESSING,
ENOUGH FOR
10 CUPS / 250 G
SALAD GREENS

1 tablespoon strong
Dijon mustard

2 tablespoons red
wine vinegar

½ teaspoon
fine sea salt

Freshly ground
black pepper

6 tablespoons
extra-virgin oil(s)
of your choice

Optional additions

2 tablespoons finely
diced **shallot**

1 **garlic** clove,
finely chopped

Fresh **herbs** (flat-leaf
parsley, chives,
cilantro, basil,
chervil), finely
chopped

1 teaspoon drained
capers, finely
chopped

CLASSIC VINAIGRETTE
Vinaigrette classique

This is the mother of all salad dressings, one you can make in any quantity and without a recipe if you remember this: one part mustard to two parts acid to six parts oil, mixed in this order, creates a velvety and well-balanced vinaigrette for crudités, salads, and steamed vegetables.

Although red wine vinegar is the classic acid to use, any vinegar or citrus juice may be substituted. Likewise, use any oil or oils that you like, but if you want to feature one that's strong-flavored, such as walnut or hazelnut, combine it with a more soft-spoken one.

1. In a small bowl, or in the salad bowl you'll use to serve your salad, combine the vinegar and salt. If you're using diced shallot and/or garlic, add it now and let it sit in the vinegar for 30 minutes to soften its edge.

2. Add the mustard and stir until blended. Add a generous grind of black pepper and then pour in the oil in a slow stream, whisking it in to emulsify. Stir in the herbs and/or capers, if using. Taste and adjust the seasoning.

HONEY LEMON VINAIGRETTE

Vinaigrette au miel et au citron

MAKES ABOUT
²/₃ CUP / 160 ML,
ENOUGH FOR
14 CUPS / 350 G
SALAD GREENS

4 teaspoons honey

**1 rounded teaspoon
strong Dijon mustard**

**½ teaspoon
fine sea salt**

**3 tablespoons
freshly squeezed
lemon juice**

**⅓ cup / 80 ml
extra-virgin olive oil**

While a classic vinaigrette (opposite) can't be beat, this recipe is the one I turn to when I want something a little different. Mildly sweet from the honey and tangy from the lemon juice, it pairs well with all manner of crudités and salad greens, and it is the one I use in my Shaved Fennel Salad (page 65).

Like any vinaigrette, this takes no time at all to whip up, but feel free to make a double or triple batch, to keep in a jar in the fridge. Shake well before using to re-create the emulsion.

In a small bowl, or in the salad bowl you'll use to serve your salad, combine the honey, mustard, and salt. Whisk in the lemon juice with a fork, pouring it in slowly so the mixture remains smooth, and then whisk in the olive oil. Taste and adjust the seasoning.

MAKES 1 CUP /
240 ML

**1 large organic
egg yolk (see Note)**

**1 tablespoon
garlic-chile sauce,
or more to taste**

**1 tablespoon
freshly squeezed
lemon juice**

**½ teaspoon fine sea
salt, or more to taste**

**¾ cup / 180 ml
neutral-tasting oil,
such as grapeseed
or safflower**

CHEATER'S SPICY GARLIC MAYONNAISE
Rouille du tricheur

The French name for this sauce is *rouille*, or "rust," in reference to its dark orange color. It is classically made by pounding garlic and chile peppers to form a paste that will flavor a homemade mayonnaise. It is the traditional condiment to serve alongside a fish soup or bouillabaisse, such as Poor Man's Bouillabaisse (page 29), but it is just as good in sandwiches and potato salads.

Making your own mayonnaise is much faster and easier than is generally thought and it is also intensely rewarding. I do, however, save myself the pounding step, and flavor it with a ready-made garlic and chile sauce, such as Harissa (page 212) or Sriracha.

Olive oil is too assertive to play solo in a mayonnaise, but you can include a few tablespoons if you want to.

1. Bring all the ingredients to room temperature before you begin.

2. Set a medium bowl on a dampened kitchen towel on the counter to keep it steady. In the bowl, whisk together the egg yolk, garlic-chile sauce, lemon juice, and salt.

3. Measure the oil into a measuring cup with a pouring spout. Pour it into the bowl a few drops at a time at first, whisking constantly to allow the oil to form an emulsion with the other ingredients. Whisk with your dominant hand and pour the oil with the other; the bowl should not move, thanks to the dampened towel.

4. When the mixture becomes creamy, you can start pouring the oil in a very thin drizzle, whisking all the while. When all the oil has been added, the mayonnaise should form peaks.

5. Taste and add a little more salt or garlic-chile sauce as needed. Transfer to a jar with a tight lid, refrigerate, and eat within the next 2 days.

note Because the egg yolk in mayonnaise is not cooked, use the freshest egg you can find. Even so, pregnant women, young children, and people with a weakened immune system should avoid eating foods that contain raw eggs.

1 large organic egg,
hard-boiled (see
page 110), peeled

1½ teaspoons strong
Dijon mustard

⅛ teaspoon fine
sea salt

⅓ cup / 80 ml
neutral-tasting oil,
such as grapeseed
or safflower

2 tablespoons /
30 ml extra-virgin
olive oil

1 teaspoon white
wine vinegar or cider
vinegar (optional)

1 cup / 20 g fresh
herb leaves (such
as a mix of parsley,
tarragon, chervil,
and dill)

2 tablespoons
capers, drained
and finely chopped

1 tablespoon finely
chopped cornichons
(optional)

GRIBICHE SAUCE
Sauce gribiche

Gribiche is an old word used in the Swiss French dialect for an
ugly witchlike woman who is called upon to scare kids into doing
things, but it's hard to see the connection with this innocent
little sauce. Sauce gribiche starts out like a mayonnaise, only it
is emulsified with a cooked, rather than raw, egg yolk. Capers,
cornichons, herbs, and chopped bits of cooked egg white are
folded in to create a highly flavorsome, slightly chunky sauce.

It is traditionally served with cold fish and meats, calves'
head, and beef stew, but it pairs just as well with vegetables, raw
or cooked. It is especially good with asparagus, spooned over
crisp lettuce and steamed new potatoes, or dotted on a bowl of
Roasted Roots (page 132).

1. Bring all the ingredients to room temperature before
   you begin.

2. Set a medium bowl on a dampened kitchen towel on
   the counter to keep it steady.

3. Halve the hard-boiled egg and separate the white from
   the yolk. Push the yolk through a sieve into the bowl
   (alternatively, mash it to a very fine paste with a fork).
   Mix in the mustard and salt until completely smooth.

4. Measure both oils into a measuring cup with a
   pouring spout. Pour it into the bowl a few drops at a
   time at first, whisking constantly to allow the oil to
   form an emulsion with the other ingredients. Whisk
   with your dominant hand and pour the oil with
   the other; the bowl should not move, thanks to the
   dampened towel.

5. When the mixture becomes creamy, you can start pouring the oil in a very thin drizzle, whisking all the while. When all the oil has been added, the mayonnaise should form peaks. If the sauce seems stiff, whisk in the vinegar to loosen.

6. Chop the egg white finely. Fold the egg white, herbs, capers, and cornichons (if using) into the sauce. Taste and adjust the seasoning. Transfer to a jar with a tight lid, refrigerate, and eat within the next 3 to 4 days.

note If pressed for time, make a shortcut gribiche sauce by adding finely chopped capers, cornichons, fresh herbs, and hard-boiled egg white to good-quality store-bought mayonnaise.

**5 ounces / 140 g
dried red chile
peppers, a mix
of mild and strong,
stemmed and seeded
(keep some or all of
the seeds to make
the harissa hotter)**

Boiling water

**½ teaspoon caraway
seeds or ¼ teaspoon
ground caraway**

**½ teaspoon cumin
seeds or ¼ teaspoon
ground cumin**

**½ teaspoon
coriander seeds
or ¼ teaspoon
ground coriander**

3 garlic cloves

**1 teaspoon
fine sea salt**

**6 tablespoons
extra-virgin olive oil,
or more if needed**

HARISSA

Harissa is a ubiquitous condiment in North African cuisine.
A purée of chile peppers mashed with garlic and spices, it is
typically served with couscous, such as Couscous with Vegetables
(page 124), or used as a sandwich spread. It can also spice up
salads, such as Eggplant and Fresh Herb Tabbouleh (page 69),
and sauces, such as Cheater's Spicy Garlic Mayonnaise (page
208), act as a spice rub, and step in anywhere you might use
strong mustard.

We consume a lot of the stuff at home; on the handful of
occasions I've traveled to Tunisia or Morocco, I've brought back
tubs of it, purchased at bustling corner stores where they ladle it
out from large barrels. When that runs out, I either get more at
the supermarket, where it is sold in toothpaste-like tubes, or mix
my own from dried chiles for fresher and more vibrant results.

1. In a heatproof bowl, cover the chile peppers with
   boiling water. Set aside for 15 minutes to soften.

2. In a small skillet, combine the caraway, cumin, and
   coriander and toast over medium heat stirring often to
   prevent burning, until fragrant. Let cool completely.
   If you're using whole seeds, grind in a spice grinder or
   with a mortar and pestle.

3. Drain the chile peppers and pat dry with a kitchen
   towel. Transfer to a food processor or blender and add
   the ground spices, garlic, salt, and olive oil and process
   until completely smooth, scraping down the sides
   regularly. Add a little more oil as needed to make the
   mixture smooth. Taste a tiny dab on a piece of bread (it
   may be hotter than you think) and adjust the seasoning.

4. Transfer to a jar and use within a month.

BÉCHAMEL SAUCE
Sauce béchamel

Named after Louis de Béchamel, the seventeenth-century gourmet who was Louis XIV's maître d' and may have been its inventor, béchamel is a milk-based sauce thickened with flour. It comes into play in many French dishes and is an oft-used component in vegetable gratins, such as Cauliflower Gratin with Turmeric and Hazelnuts (page 171).

Although the idea of making a sauce from scratch can sound intimidating to the beginner cook, there is little to worry about here; so long as you can whisk and watch, you'll have a silky béchamel ready in minutes. The classic version calls for butter and cow's milk, but it can be made vegan by substituting oil and nondairy milk. Have all the ingredients measured out and ready before you begin.

MAKES 1⅓ CUPS / 320 ML BÉCHAMEL SAUCE

2 tablespoons / 30 g unsalted butter, or 2 tablespoons neutral-tasting oil, such as grapeseed or safflower

3 tablespoons / 25 g all-purpose flour

1⅓ cups / 320 ml milk (not skim) or unflavored, unsweetened nondairy milk

½ teaspoon fine sea salt

Freshly ground black pepper

Freshly grated nutmeg

1. Melt the butter or heat the oil in a medium saucepan over medium heat. When the butter starts to sizzle or the oil to shimmer, add the flour and whisk it in (this is called a *roux blanc*). Cook, stirring constantly with the whisk, until creamy but not colored, about 3 minutes.

2. Pour in the milk, little by little, whisking it into the roux, watching out for any clumps on the bottom and sides of the pan. Bring to a simmer and cook for a few minutes, stirring as the mixture becomes creamy, like a thin custard sauce. Dip a wooden spoon in the béchamel and run your finger along the back of it: if the trace remains clear, the sauce is done.

3. Season with salt, pepper, and a whisper of nutmeg. Use immediately.

¼ cup / 80 g good-quality all-natural tahini

2 tablespoons chopped fresh herbs (such as chives, cilantro, parsley, and mint)

1 teaspoon freshly squeezed lemon juice

½ garlic clove, pressed in a garlic press or finely chopped

¼ teaspoon fine sea salt

Freshly ground black pepper

HERBED TAHINI SAUCE
Sauce tahini aux herbes

Tahini, a Middle Eastern sesame paste, can be thinned into a quick sauce that is traditionally served over falafel. Its flavor is rich but bright, and its subtle nuttiness enhances the other elements on the plate like magic.

It goes superbly well with vegetables—steamed, sautéed, or roasted—such as carrots, broccoli, winter squash, or root vegetables (see page 132), and with legumes, such as Lentil Croquettes (page 176).

In a bowl, combine the tahini, herbs, lemon juice, garlic, salt, and pepper. Stir in a few drops of cold water. When mostly incorporated, add a few drops more and repeat. The tahini should be thinned little by little to avoid curdling. As you add the water, the mixture will change in consistency and color, from grainy to smooth, and from beige to off-white. Add about 2 tablespoons to make it thick and creamy for a dip, or 3 tablespoons to make a thin and milky sauce. Taste and adjust the seasoning.

SHELL-POACHED EGGS
Oeufs pochés en coquille

MAKES 6 EGGS

**6 large organic eggs,
at room temperature**

Hervé This is a French researcher who explores the physical and chemical aspects of cooking. Among his popular experiments is "the 65-degree egg," based on the observation that the white and yellow parts of the egg set at different temperatures. Therefore he suggests cooking eggs in their shell in the middle of that temperature range, at 150°F. / 65°C., to obtain a set white and a creamy yolk, as the Japanese have long done with their *onsen tamago*, an egg plunged in natural hot springs to cook.

This technique requires a thermometer to control the water temperature in the saucepan, but the result is a soft-boiled egg with a marvelously silky, almost slippery white—unlike the stiff texture you get from boiling the egg—and a custardy yolk. Serve these eggs on slices of toast, in cups of soup, or in bowls of warm vegetables, such as in Poor Man's Bouillabaisse (page 29).

1. Fill a medium saucepan with water and clip an instant-read food thermometer to the inside. Bring the water to a temperature of 150°F. / 65°C.

2. Lower the whole eggs in gently, cover, and set the heat to the lowest possible setting underneath the pan, keeping an eye on the thermometer to make sure the water remains at the temperature given above. It can vary by a few degrees up or down, but you should err on the side of cool, and the temperature should not go over 155°F. / 68°C. or the yolk will set. If the temperature seems about to rise too much, remove the pan from the heat and add a little cold water as needed.

RECIPE CONTINUES

3. Cook the eggs for 45 minutes, the time it takes for the egg white to coagulate, while the yolk remains custardy.

4. To serve, crack each egg into a small bowl—it will slip right out of the shell—then tilt the bowl and slide the egg onto the dish you want to garnish with it. You can also let the eggs cool, in the shell, and refrigerate for up to 2 days; if desired, reheat by plunging the eggs in a bowl of hot water for 5 minutes.

note Alternatively, if your oven is well calibrated and offers the option of a low temperature, put the eggs (in the shell) in a baking dish, and cook them in the oven preheated to 150°F. / 65°C. for 45 minutes.

LEMON PASTRY CREAM
Crème pâtissière au citron

MAKES ABOUT
1 CUP / 240 ML,
ENOUGH FOR A
10-INCH / 25 CM
TART

Pastry cream is a thick custard used in French pastry to fill fruit tarts and turnovers, cream puffs, and éclairs. It is similar to pudding—and just as easy to make.

I use this lemon version in Strawberry Tartlets (page 48), but once you get the hang of the basic method, you can dream up any flavor variation you like: vanilla, chocolate, pistachio, rose, and so on.

1. In a medium bowl, whisk together the egg, sugar, and cornstarch.

2. In a medium saucepan, bring the milk and lemon zest to a simmer over medium heat. Slowly whisk the hot milk into the egg, and then pour the egg-milk mixture back into the saucepan.

3. Return to low heat and whisk constantly for 1 minute as the mixture thickens to a custardy consistency, making sure to scrape the sides and bottom of the pan regularly so the texture is even. Dip a wooden spoon in and run your finger along the back of it: if the trace remains clear, the pastry cream is done.

4. Pour into a clean bowl and whisk in the lemon juice. Cover, pressing a piece of plastic wrap onto the surface of the custard, and refrigerate for a few hours until chilled. The pastry cream may be prepared up to a day in advance; whisk again before using.

1 large organic egg

3 tablespoons unrefined blond cane sugar (also sold as evaporated cane juice)

2 tablespoons cornstarch

⅔ cup / 160 ml milk (not skim) or unflavored, unsweetened nondairy milk

Grated zest of 1 organic lemon

¼ cup / 60 ml freshly squeezed lemon juice

ACKNOWLEDGMENTS
Remerciements

I'd like to thank **Maxence**, first and foremost, for loving vegetables as much as I do, for tasting my cooking experiments with unfailing enthusiasm, and for being my most trusted, yet most gentle, critic.

Heaps of gratitude to my friend **Mary Sue Hayward**, the best and wittiest recipe tester ever, whose thorough and entertaining notes were an invaluable help.

Heartfelt thanks to **Emilie Guelpa** (aka Griottes) for the wonderful photos of Paris and its prettiest greenmarkets, and to photographer **Françoise Nicol** and food stylist **Virginie Michelin** for creating such vibrant images of my recipes.

Thank you, also, to **Isabelle Poupinel** for letting us use some of her gorgeous handmade porcelain dishes as props (pages 109, 113, 117, 120, 125, 129, 141, 147, 150, 158, 164, 178, and 191), and to **¿adónde?** as well, whose clean-line plates I adore (pages 19 and 21).

For the better part of a decade, I have had the incredible good fortune of working with my agent and friend, **Claudia Cross**; receiving her support and guidance for this book has felt wonderful, as ever.

Many thanks to the team at Clarkson Potter, and especially **Rica Allannic, Rae Ann Spitzenberger, Terry Deal, Kim Tyner,** and **Ashley Phillips,** for bringing this book to life with such flair and passion.

To the **readers of *Chocolate & Zucchini***, I want to express my gratitude, too, for reading my words year after year, and for being the most engaging and supportive audience a writer could hope for.

A final word in loving memory of my grandmother, **Mamy**, who left before she could see this book in print, but has inspired so many of its pages.

HUNGRY FOR MORE?

Log on to the *Chocolate & Zucchini* website (http://chocolateandzucchini .com) for regular updates, bonus content, and more recipes. You can also e-mail the author at clotilde@clotilde.net.

RECIPE INDEX

Note: Page references in *italics* indicate photographs.

Appetizers

Soups

Salads

Savory tarts

Main courses

INDEX

Note: Page references in *italics* indicate photographs.